50 Ways to Be
Better Speaker

ADEBAYO'S
KOPI

# 50 Ways to Become a
# Better Speaker

Douglas Kruger

**Mindex** Publishing
COMPANY LIMITED
*Benin *Abuja * Lagos * Aba *Nigeria.
T: 08054755695, 08023453848, 08037404398

50 ways to Become a Better Speaker
© 2006 by Douglas Kruger

All rights reserved under the Pan-American and International Copyright Conventions. This book may not be reproduced, in whole or in part, in any form or by any means electronic or mechanical, including photocopying, recording, or by any information storage and retrieval system now known or hereafter invented, without written permission from the publisher, Mindex Publishing Co. Ltd.

This Edition is Published under exclusive license
( Not for Sale Outside Nigeria) with the permission of
NB Publishers (Pty) Limited, South Africa
By Mindex Publishing Company Limited.
7 Obaroghedo Street, Off Benin Technical College Rd.,
Ugbowo, Benin City, Edo State, Nigeria.
Tel: 08054755695, 08023453848, 08037404398
E-mail: mindexpc@yahoo.com    www.mindexpublishing.com

ISBN 978 - 978 - 48185 - 8 - 2

*Marketed by:*

*Mindex Bookshops*

*Abuja:* 4, Peter Okorunmadu Street, Garki II Model Market, Garki II, Abuja. Tel: 08072250747
*Lagos:* 20, Bale Street, Apapa-Ajegunle Boundary, Ajegunle, Lagos. Tel: 08057377240
*Aba:* Shop 112B, Line F. Ariaria Market, Aba. Tel: 08025686984
*Benin City:* 85, New Lagos Rd., New Benin, Benin City. Tel: 08033786116
Also available in all leading Bookshops nationwide.

*Printed in Nigeria by:* Mindex Press Limited. Benin City.
Tel: 08054755695, 08023453848, 08037404398

# Contents

**Introduction**    7
**Setting the scene**    9
   Nightmare in tender land – a true story    9
**The 50 ways**    13
  1.  Make sure *you* should be speaking    13
  2.  Role-play the day, step by step    14
  3.  Make sure your audience know why they are there    15
  4.  Handle matters when tragedy strikes    16
  5.  Attend the talk just before your own    18
  6.  Bring along your own introduction    20
  7.  Find out about your audience in advance    21
  8.  Arrange your speaking aids/room beforehand    23
  9.  Grab your audience's attention    26
10.  Establish rapport during 'getting-to-know-you' time    29
11.  Tell the audience what to expect    30
12.  Speak with purpose    31
13.  Design your content to pass the 'who cares?' test    32
14.  Inject life into your voice    33
15.  Be wary of insulting your audience    36
16.  Give your audience permission to laugh    37
17.  Build climaxes into your speech    39
18.  Speak in the active voice    42
19.  Command your environment    43
20.  Ignore the cameras    48
21.  Manage your hand-outs wisely    49
22.  Make sure *you* are the attraction, not your slide show    51
23.  Speak to your audience 'where they are at'    53

| | |
|---|---|
| 24. Keep your audience with you | 55 |
| 25. Speak with vibrancy | 59 |
| 26. Control nervous tics and twitches | 61 |
| 27. Be wary of crutch words | 63 |
| 28. Rehearse your speech while writing it | 65 |
| 29. Appeal to the imagination | 67 |
| 30. Turn your points into stories | 71 |
| 31. Use 'we' instead of 'you' | 73 |
| 32. Speak as if to a single person | 74 |
| 33. Avoid paralanguage | 75 |
| 34. Deliver emotion tactfully | 76 |
| 35. Use pauses consciously and often | 77 |
| 36. Don't hide behind notes | 79 |
| 37. Use an essay style rather than lists | 81 |
| 38. Always walk your talk | 82 |
| 39. Use pictures and stories to make your numbers meaningful | 83 |
| 40. Listen to your audience | 85 |
| 41. Be spontaneous | 86 |
| 42. Use rhythm and contrast | 92 |
| 43. Deliver a toast with panache | 92 |
| 44. Maintain total control over Q&A | 94 |
| 45. Repeat questions from the audience | 94 |
| 46. Slot in Q&A at the three-quarter mark | 95 |
| 47. Avoid verbal cues | 97 |
| 48. End on a 'professional' note | 98 |
| 49. Stay after your presentation | 103 |
| 50. Have an encore prepared | 105 |
| **Summary of action items** | **106** |
| **Being a perpetual student** | **110** |
| **Troubleshooting** | **114** |
| **Super-effective speaking** | **117** |
| **Speaker's checklist** | **126** |
| **Becoming a professional speaker** | **128** |
| **Final thought** | **141** |
| **About the author** | **143** |

# Introduction

Do you often speak in public? Do you wish to become a better speaker? And do you believe that we need not reinvent the wheel? Then this book is for you – whether you are a novice speaker, a person required to give business presentations or a full-time professional wishing to hone your skills

Besides giving expert advice on how to become a professional, I set out 50 ways in which you can become a more effective speaker – by avoiding common pitfalls and elementary mistakes and by adopting a variety of techniques that will give your speeches authority and polish.

Public speaking can be a scary business. Your margin for error is surprisingly wide when you consider that your mistakes are witnessed by a living, breathing and laughing audience. If you really botch up, it may affect your reputation or your sales. It could diminish your credibility as a leader. It may be felt in your *career*.

So, let's shorten your learning curve. In this book you will encounter actual examples where speakers have blundered, belittled their audience or bludgeoned them into boredom – and ultimately lost the attention of those whom they sought to persuade.

Some of the lessons have been mine, learnt the hard way in the course of building a professional speaking career; while others derive from the errors of speakers and presenters whom I have watched and zealously analysed over the years. I recount these incidents to save you from making the same embarrassing mistakes we did.

Rather than focus on the negative, however, in each case I explore what *could* have been done, and suggest how *you* can do it better. Because at some stage in your life, you will *have* to speak publicly. It may happen informally or when you're called on to make a formal business presentation or asked to speak at a family wedding.

Whatever the occasion, I want your audiences to listen to you. To *really* listen. I want them to consider your words attentively, be persuaded by your logic and, above all, to enjoy listening to you.

The advice given in this book ranges from problems that may arise during the preparation of your speech and the arrangements around its delivery. It proceeds through the dangers and difficulties you might face in mid-speech, as you perform before a critical or dozing audience. And it ends with the all-important *conclusion* of your presentation, by which point you will either have won over your listeners or sent them to sleep, depending on the quality of your presentation.

Each of the 50 ways to become a better speaker contains a suggested technique that will help you to produce results. Some of these techniques are my own; others are tips gathered from highly accomplished international speakers.

Take note of them. Use them. And keep them in mind every time you speak in public. So that people will listen attentively to what you have to say ...

Good luck!

*Douglas Kruger*

# Setting the scene

## Nightmare in tender land – a true story

## 3

The morning I began writing this book, I watched a woman throw away millions in potential revenue for her company. I drove home to my PC and recorded the details while they were fresh in my memory. Here's what happened.

Thembi was the head of a highly successful training company. She had invited me to sit in on a tender bid for new business, to observe how she performed and provide her with feedback. The client was a multinational company, and the potential fee was huge. She was down to the final pitch, the deciding presentation . . . the moment when her speaking skills could make or break her.

Her company had been short-listed as one of four, out of 240 applicants. Her credentials were right, her business connections impeccable and her references, without exception, *outstanding*.

And so, with all of Thembi's proverbial ducks in a row, the two of us arrived at the company's headquarters. The ingredients for a killer presentation were there, and her confidence was high. Clasping her laptop – with me in tow – Thembi walked into the room. And to an unpleasant surprise . . .

The empty boardroom she'd expected was anything *but* empty. Eight panel members were already seated and waiting. They had been there for the past two hours, listening to the previous presentation.

Thembi had no time to gather her thoughts or set up her laptop. Hers was a live performance, which had just begun. She scuttled awkwardly down the side of the room, greeting people as she jostled by. Thrown by this unexpected development, she forgot to introduce me. So I greeted everyone myself, explained my presence, and took a seat.

The room was hot and stuffy and the panel members were tired, in need of a break. All the tell-tale signs were there: elbows rested on table, chins on hands, coffee mugs were empty and glazed eyes betrayed a desire to get into the fresh air – if only for a few minutes.

But Thembi wasn't *reading* the signs. While unpacking her laptop, she became aware that all eyes were upon her. So to divert attention, she handed out printed copies of her slides.

She had stapled together thick wads of A4 pages, with four slides printed on each page – so small that we couldn't make out the bullet points – and had prepared no fewer than 99 individual slides. Each one bore six or seven separate bullet points: enough to cause brain damage to the most diehard PowerPoint junkie.

Thembi's laptop had a two-pin plug, but she didn't have an adapter. One of the panel members was kind enough to walk to the next office and retrieve one for her. As her laptop started whirring slowly into life, she tried to make small talk. But half the panel members were squinting at the slides on her paper, ignoring her completely. Then she asked where the projector was . . .

'Oh,' one of the weary panel members answered, 'we don't have a projector. Didn't you bring one?' There was a hint of irritation in his voice.

Thembi was beginning to panic. She turned to me, 'Could you please go and get the Proxima from my car?' Given the pressure she was under, I obliged as quickly as I could.

Then the laptop had to be switched off so that the projector could be connected. Then it had to be rebooted.

And all of this in front of an increasingly agitated audience.

Thembi was starting to perspire and her voice began cracking at the edges as she murmured about 'what a hassle technology can be'. Then the laptop froze. It got halfway to booting up, and simply froze. Under her breath, but loud enough for the entire room to hear, she hissed an obscenity.

By this stage, we had lost 25 of our allocated 45 minutes. And panel members were moving around in their chairs, exchanging glances.

I leaned over and whispered, 'Why don't you just go on without the slides?' But the very idea was foreign to her. She was utterly dependent on them. Another attempt brought the obstreperous machine to life, and with that the presentation finally began.

Slowly and relentlessly, Thembi began working her way towards slide no 99. She read each slide *word for word*. She didn't stop to ask questions or to check that everyone understood. The language was pure 'corporate-speak', riddled with 'visions' and 'missions' and 'strategic alignments', with not the slightest attempt to humanise the content.

I felt genuinely sorry for those poor people. *And for myself.* What had we done to deserve this? What she was doing was burying a room full of living, feeling human beings in dull, uninteresting verbiage.

All the advantage Thembi had gained because of her credentials, she quickly lost through poor presentation skills. She jeopardised any hope of winning that bid simply because she looked unprepared and unprofessional, and failed to build any rapport with her evaluators. Thembi is actually a highly professional individual who put a great deal of work into her preparation, as evidenced by the abundance of carefully prepared slides. What's more, she is a very warm person, and easy to like. It's a great pity the panel never got to see that.

So what went wrong?

Thembi made several fundamental mistakes that all of us could easily make too. They are very common and were made because she was an undereducated presenter. There were many things she could have done to improve the situation.

For example, when she first walked into the room and saw everyone seated, she could have asked politely if they would like a five-minute comfort break while she set up. They would have jumped at the chance to stretch their legs. She could have done all her preparation and back-pedalling without an ogling audience, who, when they returned to the room, would have been much more receptive to her message. And she would have come across as calm and unflustered.

She could also have forsaken her slides entirely and simply spoken with passion and conviction about what made her company special. She knew her pitch backwards and forwards. It's *her* company, after all. As it happened, she might as well have e-mailed the slides to each panel member to read, as she didn't say a thing that wasn't already written down. She could even have asked the panel members outright which aspects they were most interested in hearing about, and then addressed those critical areas *only*.

There are so many things Thembi *could* have done. But the moment had come and gone for her. And so, unfortunately, had the fee associated with it.

When will the 'moment' be upon you; and what will be at stake when it arrives? Would you like the peace of mind that comes with adequate preparation? Would you prefer not to have to grind your teeth and swear beneath your breath when you have to stand up and speak?

Then let's get cracking, and, like Freudians, anticipate our worst nightmares as a speaker. Once we better understand our fears, they can be made to vanish into the mist. Public speaking can be both enjoyable and profitable – if done well.

I suggest 50 ways in which you can become a better, and perhaps even a great, speaker. Each suggestion deals with a potential trap for the inexperienced speaker, but offers a way out for one who knows the ropes.

So here goes . . .

# The 50 ways

## Make sure you should be speaking       1

Even before you begin to prepare a speech, ask yourself if you really believe in what you are going to say. Honestly. Is there anything about your speech that might be dishonest, untrue or tasteless?

I once met a woman who was asked to find a motivational speaker to pep up her company's staff. When she was unable to find a suitable person, her boss asked her to do the speech herself. She was aware that a series of retrenchments were looming within the company, and hated working there herself – a fact that was well known among the staff. Nevertheless, she agreed to speak.

How much of a motivating force do you suppose she was?

For starters, the staff didn't believe the things she said – they all knew how she spoke about the company 'behind the scenes'. Secondly, when retrenchment time did come around, her credibility and believability sank even lower as staff realised that her inspirational message had been a deception.

If you are ever asked to deliver a message you don't believe in – be it a sales pitch, a motivational talk, honouring a cause, or any other form of presentation – be honest with whoever invited you. Tell him or her that you are not the right person for the job, and allow someone else to do it. You could actually harm the cause, as well as your own credibility, if you go ahead. And credibility can't be bought back easily.

There are also certain presentations which, by their nature, should be made by the most senior levels of management, even if your speaking skills are better than theirs.

You might be the PR person in your company, with a splendid track record in front of the media. But you may not be the right person to be doing the speaking. During a crisis, the CEO should be up there. So, start by determining whether *you* really are the right person to be giving the speech.

## 2 Role-play the day, step by step

In our opening story, Thembi hadn't foreseen the prospect of walking into a room full of people sitting and watching her. She also hadn't really prepared any kind of introduction. She had nothing more than slides with her.

So let's anticipate how your presentation might begin. You cannot, for starters, stand up in front of an audience, whom you have caught cold, and start reading out 'slide number one, bullet point number one', etc. You need to start somewhere else. Thembi would have foreseen this problem, and thought of a proper introduction, had she conducted a role-play beforehand.

Run through your presentation in your mind's eye well before the time. Be thorough and start with your arrival at the venue. Ask yourself, 'what will I have to do first?' Your most likely answer is something like: plug in my laptop.

This already raises a few basic questions: Do you have the right type of plug? Will you need an extension cord? Is there time on the agenda for you to set up before your presentation, or should you arrive before the day's proceedings and set up in advance? Will anyone be present to help you?

Cover every aspect of your presentation in your mind's eye, from beginning to end, and make a habit of it. But remember that the single most critical part to role-play is your *introduction* – the actual words you plan to use when you start talking.

This is the 'tone-setter', and is consequently one of the most important elements to rehearse. Practise it over and over again. A good start will set you at ease, gain the audience's attention and help ensure a successful presentation.

## Make sure your audience know why they are there  3

If you are billed in advance as a speaker, you may well grow increasingly nervous as those dreaded moments draw near, moments which – to many people – are worse than military service or root-canal treatment.

Yet audiences are often blissfully unaware of what is going on in a speaker's mind.

At an early stage in my career, I was asked to speak to a division of a large banking group in Johannesburg. To say that I was nervous would be an understatement. 'Basket case' would be closer to the mark.

As the staff ambled into the auditorium, I recall one of them asking, 'So, what's this all about, then?' At that point I realised that my listeners had no idea why they were there. Their manager had ordered them to be in the auditorium at a certain hour, and they had simply obeyed.

Why should that pose a problem, you ask? It's a problem because it means you have an audience that is distracted. People haven't arrived with any sense of anticipation or respect for the event, because they don't know why they are there. Many are surreptitiously looking at their watches and wondering how long it will be before they can get back to *real* work.

Certain types of presentations may allow you to send a short teaser to your audience in advance. If you can, go ahead and do so. Say, for example, you will be speaking to a corporate audience for an hour on sales. You might send an advance e-mail to their manager and ask him or her to pass it along. Something like: 'Tuesday afternoon will be your chance to learn how to double your sales. My name is Ted, and I look forward to meeting you then. Bring a pen, so that you can jot down my Nine Secrets of Sales Success.'

You may even create a little hype beforehand. I once conducted a training seminar on a particularly dry topic: the *pension fund surplus*. To create some degree of anticipation, I arranged to have two minutes on the agenda of a general staff meeting, one week before the training. I showed up carrying an orange in my hand, walked in and greeted the group, and threw the orange to someone in the front row. I asked him to throw it to someone else. To growing laughter and excitement, the orange did the rounds across the room, until it arrived back in my hands. By this stage, I had their undivided attention.

'What did you just have in your hands?' I asked.

'An orange!' they shouted.

'No. In fact, it's R80 billion! And next week, I will tell you why ... I ' And with that, I walked out. I had introduced myself effectively and created a sense of anticipation of things to come.

Of course, you may not always have the luxury of introducing yourself beforehand, in person or by e-mail. So in a situation where you are asked, 'What's this all about then?' your response should be to have the MC drum up a little enthusiasm about your speech. Ask him or her to tell your audience what your talk is about, make it sound exciting, and let those present know what they will get out of it. If you don't have an MC, do it yourself. Keep your enthusiasm and energy levels high, tell your listeners what they are in for, and get them excited about the ride!

## 4 Handle matters when tragedy strikes

What happens if somebody has a heart attack just before your presentation? What if an international tragedy, on the scale of 9/11, becomes known to your audience just before you rise to speak? What happens if the Boks have just lost a rugby test?

It can happen (even occasionally in the case of the Boks!)

I was in church once when an elderly gentleman, one of the deacons and a well-known personality, suffered a heart attack. He was attended to in his pew and then carried out on a stretcher. The mood among the 800-plus congregants became sombre.

This presented a dilemma for the pastor. If he were to begin his sermon as planned, he would risk looking callous and uncaring. He would also battle to hold the attention of the congregation. Yet if he digressed for too long, he might not get around to the sermon he had prepared.

As it turned out, the pastor handled the situation exceptionally well. Rather than gloss over the incident, he asked the audience to bow their heads in prayer for the old man. This not only showed respect for the situation, but provided the congregation with something constructive to do while the paramedics went about their work outside.

He then cleverly linked the incident to the content of his sermon, making no attempt at levity and keeping his tone serious and subdued. The disruption was smoothly and expertly handled.

If a tragedy occurs, resist any attempt at humour – it will only make you appear callous. If you must lighten the situation, never try to be funny about the tragedy at hand. That is guaranteed to give offence. Pick on something else instead.

Honour the seriousness of the situation by going into 'dignified' mode. In other words, speak sincerely and adopt a more formal and serious tone. And be brief. Your audience will naturally want to talk about what has happened, among themselves and with friends and family, after you've spoken. So say only what needs to be said, and sit down.

If at all possible – especially in the case of a day-long event – provide regular updates, so that your audience will not be tempted to leave or seek out information on their own.

It's unfortunate, but this is not an occasion when the audience will respond well to efforts to make them relax. Don't take it personally. In the circumstances, all that can be expected of you is to get the job done as quickly as possible – and let your audience go on their way.

# 5 Attend the talk just before your own

Even worse than having a tragedy precede your presentation, is to speak before an audience that has just been taken to task by management.

Clive Simpkins, a well-known local speaker, recalls an occasion when an audience appeared to have frozen in their seats. He had arrived to deliver his presentation to a group of sales people (usually a rowdy lot by nature), walked onto the stage to a bare minimum of applause, and begun to present.

Within moments he became aware that the audience was not responding to him at all. He tried humour, but was met with silence. He tried to appeal to their emotions, but they sat stony-faced. He tried to excite their imaginations, to no avail. A tumbleweed blew across the stage and a lone coyote howled in the distance, somewhere beyond the registration kiosk.

'I may as well have been speaking in a morgue,' he told his peers at a meeting of the National Speakers Association of South Africa. 'It made absolutely no sense to me at all.'

Clive considered giving up halfway through the talk, but after an inner tussle with himself, forged ahead and completed the presentation. But he left the venue, deeply shaken. His presentations had *always* been well received in the past and he'd put a great deal of effort and preparation into this one. *So what*, he wondered, *had gone wrong?*

The next day he mustered the courage to call the conference convenor. 'Did they not approve of me?' he asked. 'I felt like I was speaking to an empty hall.'

'Oh, it's not your fault,' came the explanation. 'Just before your talk, the sales director stood up and really chewed the group out for not meeting their targets. He actually threatened to fire half of them ...'

Clive had arrived five minutes after the great 'chewing out', and had walked onto the stage, cold, with a brief to try to motivate the crowd. Is it any wonder his talk went down like a lead balloon?

Although it wasn't Clive's fault, the experience affected him badly. The same can happen in any presentation, and it's a harrowing experience to 'wither and die' in front of an unreceptive audience. Many presenters I know have sunk into depression as a result of the blow to their morale. I once interviewed a comedian who gave up his trade for three years after 'bombing' one night in public.

So what can you do to avoid this special kind of speaker's pain?

Try to be present at the talk immediately before yours. There is nothing like actually being *in* the audience to gauge its mood. Not only that, you may pick up some 'insider' jokes that could slot neatly into your own presentation.

If you are not able to sit in the audience before your turn comes to speak, ask the MC or conference convenor the following:
- What state of mind is the audience in?
- Are they tired, or are they still going strong?
- What did they have to sit through before my speech?

When you have the answers to these questions, adapt your style accordingly. If your listeners are tired, you can either give them a quick comfort break or try to hype them up by creating a little excitement. Or you could simply keep your remarks short out of consideration for them.

If they've just been taken to task by management, as in Clive's nightmare assignment, you could actually weave that into your presentation and try to dredge up some humour. You might, for instance, begin by saying, 'You think you're having a bad day? What about me – I've got to cheer you up now! Please be kinder to me than your management has been to you . . . Speaking of management . . .' (and with this, you might link in to the topic you were going to address). Your empathy should break the tension in the room, and your audience (I'll bet) will feel a little sorry for you and listen more readily. I know *I* would.

But you must be aware of the audience's state of mind before you begin. Imagine, for example, the disaster you'd have had if you'd come on strong, opening with a bold and arrogant, 'I'm gonna change the way you do business!' straight after they'd received a bollocking. Always try to get inside the mind of your listeners by becoming part of the audience before you speak.

## 6 Bring along your own introduction

The greatest discourtesy to any speaker is to introduce him or her with that unfortunate phrase, 'John Smith . . . is a person who needs no introduction.'

The fact is that *every* speaker, without fail, needs and deserves an introduction. Whether the person is a former president or simply the guy or gal from sales, rob them of an introduction and you have robbed them of respect. Worse still is the lazy approach: 'But he will tell you about himself and why he's here.'

I can't tell you how often that has happened to me. A 'non-introduction' like that deprives you of authority before you even start. Your opening note will make you sound as if you are back-pedalling, as you hasten to explain to your audience why you are standing before them. This is the worst possible note on which to begin.

Fortunately, you don't have to suffer this injustice. You can simply bring along your own introduction. Don't be shy to draft two or three short paragraphs about yourself, detailing:
- who you are
- what your area of expertise is
- what topic you are about to talk on
- why you are qualified to talk on the topic
- a few additional facts about yourself.

Hand this information to the person who will be introducing you well before the time and ask him or her to use it. Don't ever accept, 'Oh, I was going to let you introduce yourself' as a response. . . . *Ever!* Be friendly, but insist on being properly introduced. It's really the least you can expect.

And don't be afraid to use a little humour in your introduction. It helps to break the ice. I once heard a leading US trainer, Darren La Croix – who actually speaks on using humour in the corporate world – introduced with these lines:

'Darren really gets around. He has spoken to companies all over the world. And when it comes to late-night talk shows, well, let me just mention a few names: Letterman, Carson, Fergusson . . . Darren has *watched* them all!'

The line, which misleads the audience into thinking Darren had *appeared* on TV himself, got a good laugh from the audience. Can you see how easy it was to do? The introduction didn't even draw on any facts. It was simply entertaining, and an excellent opening. It ensured that we liked Darren before we'd even met him, which is a wonderful advantage for any speaker.

Should an underperforming MC give you a non-introduction, try beginning your presentation by saying, 'Actually, I feel I do need an introduction! Otherwise, why would you listen to me? Let me tell you why I am qualified to appear before you . . .'

> **Quick tip!**
> You now know how to script your own 'intra'; but did you know you can script your own 'outro' as well? If you want to sell a book or CD after your presentation or would like people to sign up for a course, go to an internet site or book you for a future event, have the MC announce this information at the end of your talk. Using an MC's 'outro' as a marketing tool is much more effective than using one's own.

# Find out about your audience in advance  7

Neglecting this rule has caught me out more times than I'd care to admit. For some strange reason, it generally happens at schools. On one occasion, I was asked to speak to a prefect body and enthusiastically prepared material on 'Leadership' that would appeal to 16- to 18-year-olds.

There was just one thing I'd not been told. I was supposed to speak to primary-school children! Instead of bright, confident and inquiring young matriculants, the group was made up of 11- and 12-year-olds. I couldn't use the notes I'd prepared as the content would have gone over their heads.

Similarly, I was once called on to present at a prestigious private school. This time I did my homework, asking the convenor whether it was a primary or a high school.

She assured me it was a high school.

Well-prepared, I arrived with all my materials and thoughts in order . . . only to discover that I was not speaking to the students at all, but to the school's senior management. Once again, I found myself having to jump through all manner of mental hoops to readjust my presentation.

I've heard similar horror stories from salespeople, who imagined that they were going to speak to someone's personal assistant, only to find they were presenting to the board, or vice versa.

Obtain clarity up front. Whenever you are invited to speak, draw up a list of questions about the audience you are about to address. These may include:

- How many people will be present?
- What are their occupations; are they all from the same industry/company?
- What is their average age?
- What is their average education level?
- Are they predominantly male or female?
- What is their home language, or ethnic group?
- What will be their mental state when you meet them? Will they just have had lunch? Alcohol? A two-hour lecture from management?
- Are there any strong taboos, or topics to avoid? (You don't want to go in armed with a string of anecdotes about hunting, only to discover that your audience is the Anti-Gun Society of SA!)
- What is the purpose of my presentation?

(For handy reference, see also the checklist on page 126.)

# Arrange your speaking aids/room beforehand  8

Many a speaker has been horrified to arrive at a venue only to discover there is no place to rest notes. This is particularly true of boardroom presentations, where there might be nothing more than the table around which delegates are seated.

Conversely, you may specifically need a large open area in which to move as you speak, only to find that the limited space is taken up by an enormous lectern.

Here again you will discover the value of role-playing your presentation, step by step, in advance. As you reach the point in your mental rehearsal where you put your notes down to begin speaking, a little voice should be asking: 'Put the notes down on *what?*'

If you feel strongly that you need a lectern, ask in advance to have one organised. If they don't have one, a tall chair will do, but turn it to its side or at an angle and stand next to it so you don't end up poised comically behind the chair.

If you don't want a lectern to get in your way, ask in advance to have it removed. Don't do this yourself, though. The MC should do it himself, or organise a sergeant-at-arms (person who controls a room) to do it. Don't ever walk up to a stage and begin by removing the lectern, or by rearranging anything else. It looks messy and unprofessional, and is not your job.

The one notable exception to this rule was demonstrated by a skilled British comedian, who used it intentionally as a humorous device. An especially large man in a bulging suit, he walked up to the stage, picked up the pencil-thin microphone stand, moved it aside and casually remarked, 'I'll move this out the way so you can see me . . .' Given his size, it brought the house down!

It can also happen that you are not given the kind of room you expected. How could this possibly affect the quality of your presentation, you might ask?

Well, I was once asked to present at the Pietermaritzburg

Chamber of Business. I had an engagement in Johannesburg earlier the same day, which meant that I had to fly down, drive to the venue, and walk into the room almost as I arrived.

As I stood waiting to be introduced, the previous speaker wrapped up his comments and walked back to his table. I then stepped up to the spot from where he had been speaking and found a surprise awaiting me.

Ordinarily, you expect to find an audience directly ahead of you. To my horror, I discovered that this audience was divided into sections – at tables in front of me, to my left and right, and even directly behind me. Not only that, the room contained several tiers, which meant that some tables were at my height, some were lower down, and some were even higher than I was.

*How on earth am I expected to address these people?* I wondered, *They seem to be everywhere!*

I did the best I could. I took the microphone off its stand, and attempted to make eye contact with everybody, as far as possible, around the room. I was particularly worried about those seated directly behind me. How could I make them feel included, or establish any kind of rapport with them, when all they could see was my back?

Thank goodness, the speech was not a complete disaster. But I felt extremely uncomfortable from beginning to end – like a circus clown trying to juggle one too many balls.

When I concluded and was being shown to one of the tables, the penny suddenly dropped. Each table had a built-in monitor and a camera had been trained on me from one of the tiers below. Had I only stood still and spoken into the camera, the audience around the room would have had a perfect view of the speaker. The organisers had solved my dilemma in advance, but I wasn't aware of it.

Try, therefore, to be at the venue well in advance of your presentation. If possible, walk around the speaking area prior to the audience's arrival. This will immediately reveal aspects you might have missed had you scrutinised the speaking area only from afar.

My own dilemma could have been resolved had I only asked the MC, while standing at the door waiting to be introduced, if there was anything I should be aware of before I began speaking. But I didn't, and paid the price.

So I urge you to speak to the organisers beforehand. Stay in touch. Ask questions – and you will not be caught out by the unexpected.

Finally, it can be useful to know in advance what type of microphone you will be expected to use. There are four basic types of microphone:
- The traditional **hand-held** microphone, which has a cord running to an amplifier, and usually rests on a stand.
- The **cordless** microphone, which is the same as a hand-held microphone, but uses a radio transmitter instead of a wire. While it can rest on a stand, it's generally taken off and wielded freely.
- The **lapel** microphone, which is also cordless. It consists of a transmitter, which clips onto your belt buckle, and a wire that runs under your jacket or shirt to a tiny clip, which fastens neatly onto your collar, tie or lapel, and picks up your voice. This frees up your hands entirely.
- The **headset**, which pop stars wear during concerts. The headphone holds a little mouthpiece in front of your lips. Many radio stations now use this type of microphone because it allows their presenters to move freely.

The type of microphone you use will affect your ability to move around, and use body language. A corded or handheld mike is extremely limiting, as it means standing in one spot if the mike is mounted on a stand, or forfeiting the use of one hand if you take the mike off its stand. But check in advance whether it's necessary to use a mike at all. An audience of under a hundred people can usually hear you without amplification, which frees you up to move around at will.

Often an event organiser or venue manager will offer you a choice of microphones. If you plan to speak from notes while standing behind a lectern (both of which I strongly discourage), then a hand-held microphone on a stand will do. But if you plan to use body language or movement, you ideally need a lapel microphone, a headset, or at least a cordless microphone. My personal recommendation is the lapel microphone, which is small and inconspicuous, and which you can simply forget about once it has been clipped to your belt and switched on. I have used headsets before, but found them cumbersome and conspicuous. It's hard to relate to an audience when you're looking like a disc jockey!

## 9 Grab your audience's attention

Real estate agents' rallies are characteristically rowdy. They are usually loaded with A-type personalities and can be a lot of fun.

At one such gathering in Johannesburg, the auditorium was set up in such a way that six or seven hundred realtors were seated on plastic chairs, facing a panel of senior officials. The latter sat in two rows, facing the audience – very much like a meeting in the old Soviet Russia.

When the first speaker concluded and sat down, the audience applauded and began to murmur among themselves, as audiences always do. Amid the talking, coughing and clapping, the second speaker, a man seated behind the table, stood up and began to speak. He made no obvious sign that he was about to do so, but just launched into his address in a fast-paced monotone. A full minute later, members of the audience stopped talking among themselves, realised that someone was speaking, and began shouting 'We can't hear you!', as well as trying to 'shush' those around them.

The second speaker's opening was a disaster. He had to walk around from behind the table to the open clearing before it, stand in front of the audience (which is what he should have done in the first place), and begin all over again.

The first minute of any speech is crucial. It sets the tone and establishes your credibility. But if your audience is not

even aware you are about to begin, you will have missed an important opportunity. So:
- Don't ever just stand up and begin. The audience will still be shuffling, talking, coughing, and thinking about the closing comments of the previous speaker. Wait until you have their undivided attention.
- Use body language to show that you are about to begin. Walk purposefully up to the front of the room and wait for the noise to die down. Stand still until you have silence and made eye contact. The simple act of standing still and waiting works beautifully.
- When you start, speak slowly for your opening sentences. Use short, easily understood sentences with long pauses in-between. This gives the audience time to adjust to your voice, digest your introduction, and settle in to listen to you. Avoid opening with a long, complicated sentence or, if you must be wordy, speak slowly and clearly. Please note that this does not mean your opening sentences should not have *energy*. They must. But they should be delivered at a pace that your audience can take in easily.

  A good strong opening might sound like this (pay particular notice to the pacing, which is intentionally done to ease audience understanding): 'Three years ago (Pause), in this very room (Pause), I made you a promise . . . ! (Pause)'.

  A bad opening might sound like this: 'At the annual general meeting held three years ago when we discussed planning for the next few years or so, I said that there were a few things we'd do before our next meetings in Cape Town and Bloemfontein.'
- Choose your opening line carefully. A dramatic statement is much more powerful than a weak line such as, 'Thank you very much for the opportunity to be here today.' If you truly want to thank the host, why not hold it until a few seconds later, or until the end of your presentation?

  You might even begin with a dramatic or provocative statement, and then leave it hanging while you greet the audience. Thereafter, you can return to the statement. I use this technique often, and it works well. Here's an example:

'Nothing succeeds like excess! (Long pause). Mr Chairman, friends, good morning. (Pause). I've always firmly believed this maxim (Pause). And I'd like to tell you why!' Do you see the pattern? Strong opening – greeting – continue with original thought. You can use a number of variations of this technique, but do be sure to start with a strong, decisive and interesting opening sentence. Deliver the words slowly and deliberately.

- Speak loudly enough to be heard. More important, speak loudly enough to convey authority. Most untrained presenters speak too softly. It's just a fact of life. Women are particularly prone to underprojecting their voices. Strangely, this is true for all the right reasons. We were raised with the idea that it's 'rude' to shout, and women are often much more sensitive to this than men. But in public speaking, being inaudible is frustrating for your audience, and therefore equally rude.

  Every one of us has, at some stage, sat at the back of a room and strained to hear a speaker mumbling in the front. Why do that to your audience? It's a discourtesy that won't win them to your side.

  A quiet voice lacks authority and credibility. Please note, though, that there is always place for the 'dramatic whisper'. This is when you drop your voice intentionally to achieve a specific effect. I am all for that. But to do an entire presentation in a mumble, or a voice that makes your audience strain to hear you, is simply unacceptable.

  In an average boardroom or small auditorium containing around twenty people, you should sound to your own ear as though you are on the brink of a shout. Don't strain your voice or sound unnatural, but speak loudly enough so as to be heard at the back.

- Pump up the volume for your opening lines. This will arouse your audience's attention, and boost your confidence. A strong start makes you sound and feel good.

- Practise speaking aloud in the room beforehand. If a microphone is available, make sure the volume is set to the correct level for your voice – in advance. Remember that an empty room doesn't swallow up sound the way a

full room does. You may need to raise the volume a notch or two. Don't bellow, but make sure you can be heard.
- If you start speaking after waiting for an hour or more, your voice may have gone cold. Take a glass of water into the venue with you – as hot as you can bear – and sip the water before you speak. This will keep you 'warmed up'. If the situation allows it, you might also chip in with comments during discussions, just to keep your voice prepared.

## 10 Establish rapport during 'getting-to-know-you' time

Every presentation relies on building up a relationship with your audience. If you don't win them over initially, you're unlikely to persuade them later to your way of thinking. But don't be scared of this aspect – *it can be a lot of fun!* A World Champion Toastmaster, Craig Valentine, strongly recommends the use of what is known as 'getting-to-know-you' time.

What is getting-to-know-you time, you ask? Picture it this way: You wouldn't walk up to a stranger in the street and say, 'You should become more focused! If you do, you'll be more effective at work! Here are eight steps you should follow . . . !' He or she would either run away or have you certified. But you *could* more readily talk like that to a person you know well, someone who trusts you.

The same applies to audiences. You're a stranger to them when you walk up to the front of the room, and are as yet unqualified in their eyes to speak to them. But in a few short sentences, by using getting-to-know-you time, you can establish enough credibility for your advice or proposals to be welcomed.

During getting-to-know-you time, you establish rapport by referring to something that is familiar to both yourself and the audience, like the venue, the host, the cold weather outside, or even the topic under discussion – something of interest to everyone.

You might relate a funny incident that happened while you were travelling to the occasion – the familiar 'something happened on the way . . .' technique. You might refer to a person in the room with whom you are acquainted.

Whatever you choose to talk about, make sure you allow the audience to see 'the real you'. Let down your guard, and show your humanity. People respond well to that.

Use humour to break the ice. A word of caution, though: When using humour, especially while people are weighing you up, pick on yourself rather than anyone else. At this early stage the audience is not yet comfortable with your cracking a joke at their expense. But they will love you for making fun of yourself.

## 11 Tell the audience what to expect

Earlier (see page 15), I discussed telling the audience why they were there. A similar imperative applies here. Your listeners may have no more awareness of the issue you are about to discuss than they do of Icelandic politics.

Never take your audience's understanding for granted. At the outset, make it clear what they should expect from your presentation. Angle it so as to make your talk sound exciting and worth their while. As in a movie teaser, tell them a little in advance about what they can expect.

Make sure you talk about the 'benefits' to them, rather than what you will be covering. There is a world of difference between the two. In the first instance, you might say, 'In the next 20 minutes, I will show you how you can completely overhaul your sales techniques, and add an extra zero to your revenue,' or even, 'You are about to learn five secrets about homemaking that can change the way you live!'

In the second instance, you would say, 'Today, I'm going to

talk about sales techniques' – which sounds dull and boring.

Always think about the *benefits* you can bring to your listeners, and tell them in advance what they will have gained by the end of your presentation.

## Speak with purpose  12

Beware of the speaker who is asked to 'say just a few words' – for he will probably say quite a few more than is necessary.

A speech with a purpose can be as short as three minutes – and still be extremely effective. A speech with no purpose can go on for eons, as the speaker feels compelled to fill time with sloppy thoughts, poor jokes and vain attempts at flattery. All he or she will succeed in doing is annoying everyone.

Don't waste people's time. Never feel tempted to 'fill minutes', as though that were somehow important.

A good speech can be only a few minutes long, yet still be remembered for years. Why? Because it had a clear *purpose*, was well developed and, when its point had been made, it ended. Exactness is the mark of a well-written speech.

Toastmasters' 1990 World Champion, Dave Brooks, suggests using a simple but surprisingly effective tool for clarifying the purpose of your speech – an ordinary business card. Write the purpose of your speech on the back of the card, in normal-sized handwriting. If you can't do it, then you don't know why you are speaking. And that is a sure sign of impending disaster.

Here are some examples of a speech's purpose:
- To inform the audience of the difficulties faced by single parents.
- To teach the audience three new techniques to improve their sales quotas.
- To raise awareness of the plight of the homeless.
- To entertain a group after dinner.

Once you've written down the purpose of your speech in *one* to *three* simple sentences (I used only single sentences in the examples above), you can then start writing it out. The advantage is that everything you write will now be subconsciously aligned to that single, simple purpose.

And here's another revolutionary suggestion: If what you thought of saying doesn't fit the purpose of the speech, cut it out. Don't be tempted to tell a joke or make a point that does not relate to the purpose of your speech.

Every good speech has a clearly defined aim. Find it, understand it, meet the objective, and you will have a winning script on your hands. Speak with a purpose. Anything else is extraneous.

This applies even to an entertaining presentation. Your 'purpose' simply becomes 'to entertain'. Anything that does not fit the bill does not belong in your speech.

## 13 Design your content to pass the 'who cares?' test

We've all sat through boring speeches and wished they would come to an end. Middle-managers and sales people are special offenders. Too often they respond to the invitation to 'say a few words' by going into mind-numbing detail about something that is generally of little relevance to anyone but themselves.

Have mercy on your audience. When I conduct training, I tell delegates that in public speaking the number one rule is: Don't be boring. Ever!

I would rather you shocked, provoked or offended than bored your audience. When you shock people, at least they pay attention.

Always make sure that the information you are presenting is absolutely necessary. If you have more than ten slides, I guarantee there is something in your presentation that need not be there.

Corporate presenters notoriously provide too much detail.

What an audience wants to know is: *What is the point? What needs to happen? And what can we do with this information?*. They do not need endless reasons and justifications, technical information or diagrams. Once again, count your words carefully and cut out the fluff.

The second way to get your speech through the 'who cares?' test, is to purposefully try to be entertaining. It may be some humour here or there, a simple anecdote to liven things up, a role-play, video clip or bit of music. It may be a game played with an audience member. It may be nothing more than your smile and enthusiastic tone of voice. But whatever it is, it must be there.

Remember that you are talking to people with emotions and imaginations, accustomed to reading fast-paced books, listening to songs on iPods and watching movies on laptops. We are no longer a generation that will tolerate two hours of bullet points. We expect something interesting from every presentation.

Even the dullest report can be livened up with a little humour, a little drama, a little *spice* . . . Our finance minister, Trevor Manuel, does this well in his budget speeches. They are riddled with asides and wisecracks and are, consequently, always a pleasure to listen to.

The trick is to care enough to build it all in beforehand.

# Inject life into your voice  14

Imagine the scene: The previous speaker has been droning on unendingly. He is speaking slowly and is barely audible. At last his talk drags to a close and the audience applauds half-heartedly. You are next on the speaking agenda.

You will find that the temptation to emulate the previous speaker's tone is surprisingly strong. Why? Because it's *safe!* It's what the atmosphere already feels like in that room, and copying it is the path of least resistance. Changing the tone would be bold, but also a little risky.

But don't ever settle for the path of least resistance. You don't want the same half-hearted applause you've just heard. You want roaring approval. You want people to sit up and take notice. And they are desperately wanting something a little more interesting.

So here is what you can do:
- Start off loudly.
- Purposefully display greater energy than the previous speaker.
- Move more. Use larger, bolder gestures. Breathe life back into the room.
- Ask a few questions to re-engage your audience's minds.
- Smile.
- Create a sense of drama and adventure; and finally,
- Speak in a natural and conversational voice.

The last point is particularly important. I often interview managers and PR people on radio. More often than not, my interviewees walk into the studio holding a set of notes. There is nothing wrong with that, and I encourage it. But every now and again, someone will try to read from their notes instead of talking to me. They will read entire paragraphs, word for word. I understand that they are trying to overcome nerves and forgetfulness, but it changes something in their voices.

When a person is reading, you can hear it. It doesn't sound at all like a natural speaking voice. And radio listeners hear it too. A reading voice sounds much more stilted; and generally, written sentences are not structured the same way as spoken ones, which is another giveaway.

On radio, I encourage people simply to talk to me. I do not ask them anything they are unprepared for. They know their area of expertise much better than I do. I really don't mind if they glance down from time to time at their facts or figures, but I can't allow an entire interview to be read. We lose listeners that way.

The same applies to public speaking. The habit of reading an entire speech off a script persists to this day, and I come across it often. There are three distinct disadvantages to doing it this way:

1. You lose rapport with your audience, because your energy is directed towards a piece of paper, not towards them.
2. Your tone of voice and sentence structure sound unnatural. It takes a highly skilled speech writer to make a script sound natural. It can be done, but it is rare.
3. You are script-bound, which means that you can't deviate from your text in order to introduce some spontaneous humour, and you can't move away from the lectern because if you do, you will lose your place.

    Moreover, if you discover at the point of delivery that something in your speech is inappropriate for this audience, or that you need to add or delete some content, you will find it more difficult to do so.

When you write your speech initially, do it first in broad outline. Let's imagine you have five or six main points to make. Write your points out, and next to each point, make a note of two or three stories or illustrations you plan to use. In ten minutes, you can script an entire hour of presentation.

Allow me to illustrate.

One of my hour-long motivational talks is titled: 'Escaping the Hamster Wheel'. It's a presentation on initiative and personal empowerment. The entire script for the speech appears on page 36.

This constitutes an hour of talking. If I had to write it out, word for word, I would probably have over 50 pages of text. But there's no need for me to do that, and you shouldn't either.

*But wait a minute . . . !*

Should I ever write out a speech in its entirety, I hear you ask? The answer is a resounding *it depends*. If you will be speaking for less than fifteen minutes, then yes, I would certainly prepare a script word for word – particularly if it were an important occasion. But if you are speaking for twenty minutes or more, then broad outlines will suffice.

Even if you have a perfectly scripted ten-minute talk, never be tempted to read it out from your piece of paper. Instead, memorise the broad areas (there will never be more than four

# 50 WAYS TO BECOME A BETTER SPEAKER

or five in a talk of this length; the ideal would be three), then simply deliver it conversationally.

You may ask: then why write it out at all? The answer is simply to clarify your own thoughts. Do this properly, and you won't even need cue cards.

I prefer never to use cue cards. They look messy, and frankly, are seldom needed. But if you feel you absolutely must have them, jot down your main points as well as one or two key facts and figures to glance at if you get stuck.

## 15 Be wary of insulting your audience

I once coached a professional speaker, who was developing a talk on 'Fear'. He's a friendly guy, and knew his content, but while going through the presentation, we discovered a few awkward remarks that were routine statements to him but could easily have put his audience's backs up.

While explaining how the nerve centre in the brain connects with the spine, he quipped, 'And hopefully all of you have spines!' Delivered in

front of a live audience, a line like this gets a sarcastic snicker at best. It's what is called a *cringe-making* statement.

Why risk distancing yourself from your audience? A quip like that serves no useful purpose, and could damage the rapport you've created. Rather leave it out.

There is also a more serious pitfall to avoid.

I was at a Toastmasters' meeting once when one of the speakers opened his presentation with a series of extremely racist jokes. Race in South Africa is a touchy subject. The general rule is: If you pick on everyone, you're okay. But this speaker didn't. He simply revealed his prejudice against a particular race, with a series of not particularly funny jokes at their expense.

What horrified me was that there were members of that race in the room. They smiled courteously, but looked uncomfortable. And we all felt extremely awkward. I couldn't wait for the speaker to sit down before he did any further damage.

Beware of making hurtful statements at the audience's expense. If you're in doubt about a statement or anecdote, and have the option of leaving it out, rather do so. Remember that the best kind of humour is at your own expense.

Be extremely wary of ethnic jokes, sexist humour or anything that might suggest that you are bigoted. You may get away with it at informal gatherings, where entertainment is the sole purpose of your presentation. But even then, if you must pick on people, pick on everyone equally, and perhaps consider wrapping up your remarks with a goodwill-generating phrase like, 'Having all kinds of people is what makes this such an exceptional country to live in.'

## Give your audience permission to laugh 16

Professional speaker and World Championship winner Craig Valentine, who coaches the effective use of humour, makes a valid observation. When you speak before an audience for the first time, they evaluate how they should react to you.

If you have positioned yourself as a serious personality, and haven't made it clear that an audience is allowed to laugh, they may not laugh. You might reach your 'funny bit' and be met by silence. You may even look around at the audience and notice that a few people are smiling to themselves, wanting to laugh, but not really daring to break the silence. Why is that? And what can you do about it?

Give your audience 'permission' to laugh at you. This applies particularly in speeches of a more serious nature. Intersperse any dry topic with the occasional flash of humour.

Your listeners will have perceived yours to be a sobering talk, and may feel that you are taking matters too seriously for them to consider laughing. It's up to you to put them at ease – by showing that you are able to laugh at yourself.

Smile as you lead up to a humorous line. Create an atmosphere of trust that says, 'It's okay to laugh – I think it's funny too.' When they do laugh, smile broadly yourself. You will quickly gain their empathy and respect.

> **Quick tip!**
>
> One advantage of using humour in a serious speech is that it doesn't matter if your joke 'bombs'. While this is bad for a professional comedian, it doesn't really matter in a solemn talk. If there's no laughter, just move on. You've lost nothing.

Here is an interesting fact about audience dynamics. Your body language, timing and manner can significantly affect the way audiences respond to you; to the point where you can actually *teach* them how to treat you.

Here's how it works: When you deliver a humorous line, you will get a certain amount of laughter. Should you launch into your next sentence midway through the laughter, people will quieten down so as not to miss the next line. And they will be more hesitant to laugh out loud at the following punch line, because you have effectively trained them to keep quiet. You have conditioned them not to laugh.

This can be deadly. Not only is laughter a sure-fire sign

that people are enjoying your talk, but their response is extremely encouraging. It's a great feeling to hear a room full of people laughing at your joke.

Always allow the audience time to laugh. Wait until the laughter is just starting to die down, and only then go on to your next line. It's that simple, yet it's not always that easy to do in practice. Why? Because as speakers we are usually nervous, and the temptation to rush is great. It takes discipline to simply stop talking and allow up to ten seconds of time to pass – not doing anything – while you indulge yourself in the laughter. If you can do this, it will improve the delivery of your funny lines immeasurably.

Comedienne Ellen DeGeneres hosted the 2005 Emmy Awards. I paid special attention to what she did while the audience was laughing at her jokes. After delivering a line, she would simply stop speaking and stand still, looking at the audience for what seemed an interminable period of time. And yet the overall effect appeared perfectly natural.

As a professional comic, she has learnt the art of waiting and letting the audience savour her lines. She allows them to get the joke and then to laugh. And finally, just as the laughter begins to die away, she launches into her next line.

Don't wait until complete silence falls. That's too late. You will lose the momentum you've built up with the audience. Begin to speak again just as the laughter starts tapering off.

## Build climaxes into your speech    17

Please pay special attention to this rule. I have seen the use of climactic rises and falls (or a lack thereof) make or break a speech. They are exceptionally important in building momentum, and carrying an audience along with you.

Let's start with a simple exercise. Think of your favourite book, a TV series you enjoy, or a good movie.

In each case, the main characters experienced a degree of

*tension* – a problem of some kind, whether physical, emotional or psychological. Without fail, every story is based on *conflict*, leading ultimately to *conflict resolution*. Sometimes it comes in a spectacular crescendo, like a car chase, or a final showdown, during which you in the audience are on tenterhooks. Without conflict, and without tension, there are no climaxes, and nothing interesting for the reader or viewer.

The same principle applies in speaking. When there is no tension in your speech – no *tension-and-release*, no *climax-and-lull* – your delivery will lack energy and your speech will sound flat.

Your speech needs ups and downs; it needs climaxes in the form of
- Verbal tension
- Motion-based tension
- Content-based tension.

Does this sound complicated? It's not. **Verbal** tension simply means varying the volume and speed of your voice. **Motion-based** tension means using faster or slower gestures, and varying the intensity of your body language at certain points in your delivery.

Both of these are directly tied to your content. If you are telling a story, or building toward an important point, your voice should become louder and your body movements more pronounced. And with practice, this will come naturally – you won't even need to think about it.

**Content-based** tension means that when you are building toward a decisive point in your text, you should start to speak progressively faster and louder, and move with greater emphasis. When you've reached your point, you should then drop your volume, slow down, relax your body language, and slowly start to rebuild towards the next point.

We are not necessarily talking about dramatic rises and falls. They should sometimes be subtle, as in a business presentation. Or they may be way over the top, as is often the case with a motivational talk, a fiery political speech, or an address at a rally. Whether pronounced or understated, however, the rises and falls *must* be there.

In the course of a presentation, you should be able to represent your tone of voice diagrammatically like this:

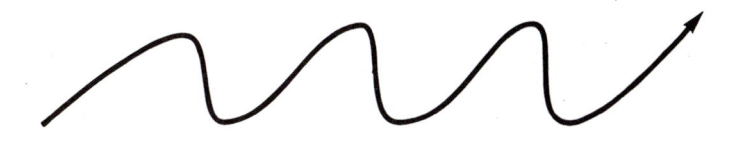

Notice that the conclusion is on an 'up' note, meaning that you should actually end with a rise in energy. (Be careful – this is not the same thing as ending an actual sentence on an up-note, which sounds dreadful.)

Reaching these high points is not difficult. They are simply the climax of the story you've been telling, the humorous line you've been building up to, or the resolution of the point you've been arguing. They are always based on your content. Once you've reached a climax in your content, stop, slow down, and then steadily begin building toward the next point.

You may even consider walking to another place on the stage, in silence, before resuming your talk. This enables you to switch naturally from the climax of one point or story to the build-up towards the next.

### Quick tip!

When structuring your speech, always use a *problem/solution* model. Don't *just* explain a great idea without any build-up to it. Instead, start by talking about the problem (conflict) that made this clever resolution necessary.

Create tension by explaining how bad the world was before this great idea came along. *Then* unleash the idea. It will be that much more effective because you have set it up properly with a negative tension.

Sales people do this all the time. They create a problem in your mind (sometimes even when you didn't know you had one), and then provide the solution: 'Did you know that dirty carpets can ruin your social life? Now, new concentrated *Blitzo* will make yours a house to be envied!'

# 18 Speak in the active voice

Let's take a trip back to your Grade 6 English class. Do you remember batty old Mrs Markham trying diligently to hammer home the difference between the active and passive voice in written English? Well, if you took the lesson to heart, Mrs Markham did you a favour. She set a standard that will forever enhance your ability to communicate.

If you stared at her blankly, wondering what was in your lunchbox, let's recap:

A sentence that lacks a subject, or fails to begin with a specific person or entity, is considered to be passive. It's the difference between saying, 'James Brown wrote this book' (active voice), and 'This book was written by James Brown' (passive voice).

Here is another type of passive sentence: 'The appropriate amount must be paid by the person buying the item.' Written in the active voice, this sentence would read, 'You must pay the appropriate amount when buying the item.'

You can instantly see that writing in the passive voice is much more formal. It is also much more difficult to process and understand quickly. Its purpose is essentially to be euphemistic, to 'soften' and to avoid offending anyone.

But it dulls an audience's minds when delivered live, simply because you as a speaker are requiring them to 'unravel' long and cumbersome sentences rather than 'absorb' them naturally.

Passive voice and euphemisms are a regrettable but all-too-common addition to modern political discourse, where the notion of addressing anybody directly is considered rude. The news on TV is awash with soggy phrases like 'it was alleged', 'it was believed', and 'measures are to be expected'. The passive voice is an ineffective way of speaking, and often a mere avoidance tactic.

If you have written your speech out word for word, scour it from beginning to end for sentences written in the passive voice. Change them to active, and see the difference it makes.

To be more precise, *feel* the difference. You should immediately sense a more energised, vigorous speech, rather like engaging the turbocharger on a car. Sluggish text becomes more focused and direct.

Look out for lines like 'it is believed that . . .', 'an analysis is to be done . . .', and 'it shall not be thought that anyone will . . .', etc. Rewrite them so that responsibility is assigned to someone, for example, 'I believe . . .', 'you must do an analysis . . .', 'please don't . . .', and so on.

If you have not written your speech out word for word, you will need to apply this technique on the fly. It's not as hard as you might think. Keep these simple guidelines in mind:
- Speak as if you are instructing a single person.
- Avoid formal phrases or euphemistic language, such as 'it should be noted that'. Instead say, 'you should note'. Talk *to* people, rather than softly tiptoeing around them.
- Ditch soggy and lifeless 'political-speak'. Avoid phrases you hear on the news such as 'in terms of' or 'it has come to light that' or 'whereas it was previously the case that . . .' and other such brain-numbers.

If you are going to say something, say it boldly and directly, and don't cloak it in verbiage. Authority comes from delivering your speech with boldness and conviction – not from hiding your meaning.

# Command your environment 19

In 2004, I was fortunate enough to win the Toastmasters' Southern African Championship for Public Speaking. A fellow contestant, wanting to improve his own speaking abilities, asked me if I could identify any one thing that set me apart from the rest.

I stumbled across the answer by accident, while watching a video of the contest. Fast-forwarding through each speech in turn, trying to find mine, I noticed something interesting. In the course of an entire speech, each contestant would move no more than a step or two to the left, and a step or two to the right. That represented the sum total of their movements on stage.

When I reached my own speech, I decided to fast forward it too. And I noticed that I moved around the stage extensively. Quite simply, I used my allotted space to greater effect. The result enhanced my 'stage presence'. I came across as 'bigger, fuller, more commanding', simply because I used my space effectively.

I'm not saying you should jump around the stage, or pace around unnecessarily. Too much movement is visually distracting, and pacing while you speak is an awful habit. But a healthy dose of controlled, purposeful movement will enhance your presence.

I was fortunate to have been tutored by the then world champion, Oregon-based Dr Randy Harvey. Dr Harvey elevated my stage craft and choreography to a new level by introducing me to the concept of 'vignettes'. These are the 'stories' you plan to tell, or the 'points' you intend to make. You use them in the following way.

Divide your speech into a series of 'vignettes'. Once you've identified them, choreograph your presentation so that you deliver each 'vignette' from a different location on stage. When you are actually speaking, stay more or less still on the spot. But when you've made your point, move to a different on-stage location and begin your next 'vignette'.

The advantage of this is that, for the audience, it mentally categorises the points you've made into different 'visual areas'. For example: Stage left is the place where you greeted the audience and gained rapport. Centre stage is the place where you introduced your topic, and put forward an argument for or against it. Stage right is where you told a supporting story. And then you came back to centre stage for your finale. All these points were neatly divided by silences (or *pauses*), immediately after the 'climax' of each point.

Let's map out a simple speech for the sake of illustration.

Pretend that you are a pilot in the air force, and your speech is on the topic 'What it's like to fly for a living'.

Your speech might have five major sections:
1. The introduction – in which you tell the audience who you are, how long you've been flying, and what flying means to you.
2. An interesting story – in which you recount a highlight in your flying career.
3. The body of the speech – in which you explain some of the intricacies of your craft, and what it takes to get to where you are.
4. Another interesting story – in which you recount a terrifying, life-threatening moment in your flying career.
5. The conclusion – in which you tell the audience about your plans for the future, and wrap up your talk.

We could map out this presentation, on a stage, as follows:

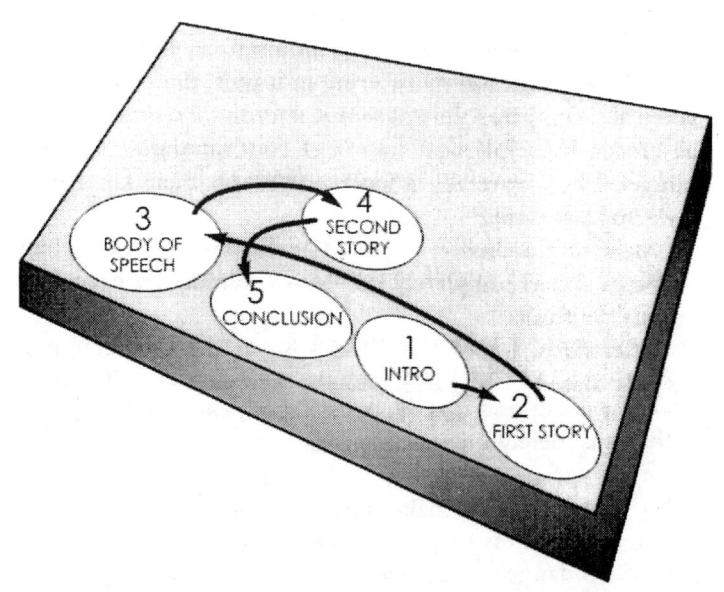

You would deliver each of these different sections from an allocated spot on the stage.

Try it for yourself. It's surprisingly effective. Plus, the few seconds in which you 'walk' between vignettes is a valuable 'bridging' period, which partitions one thought from another and helps the audience to follow your argument, besides giving you a few valuable moments to gather your thoughts. Of course, there's no need to be robotic about your use of vignettes. Think of the movement between each 'scene' as more of a ballet than a series of disjointed sections.

Now that we've looked at the stage, let's consider the surrounding environment as well. A few years ago, I learnt a lesson in public speaking the hard way. It's a lesson you won't find in many manuals.

I was well into a motivational speech at a new conference venue in Cape Town. It was a warm evening, and the audience was with me. But then, as my message built to a crescendo, the hotel staff threw a curveball my way. They served starters.

Serving starters in the middle of a speech is like belching loudly during a piano recital. The moment may pass quickly, but the atmosphere will be altered.

For a minute, there was a commotion in the room. The clinking of plates and murmuring of waiters drowned out my voice and dissipated the emotional tension I'd worked so hard to create. Eyes followed trays and concentration turned to hunger. Then, naturally, people picked up their knives and forks to start eating.

An eating audience, I quickly learned, is not a watching audience. I had completely lost their attention – except for a few in the front.

Afterwards, I took a second look at the programme. It actually stated '8:30 pm – Douglas Kruger and Starters'. Of course, I had read it as 'Douglas Kruger *and then* Starters'. But that was merely my interpretation.

So how can you make sure that nothing detracts from the effectiveness of *your* presentation? Start with the most obvious danger – our friend the cellphone. Ask your audience to double-check that their phones are off, or get the MC to do it.

Set up the room in advance. Make sure there are no wires in your way and that your audience has clear visual access to you. If anything doesn't suit your presentation style, ask to have it changed.

Speak to the people in charge. Stay in touch with the conference convenor or meeting planner, as well as the MC. Run through the order of events with them, until you understand exactly what is going to happen and in what order. If you see a potential pitfall, don't be shy to bring it up. Advise them: 'My message will be compromised *if* . . .'

Never 'interpret' the running order. Don't assume that 'John Smith *and* Starters' means 'John Smith *and then* Starters', as I did. Talk things through with your host step by step in advance: 'As I understand it, Jim will introduce me, I will speak, and after I finish, starters will be served. Is that correct?'

Even the seating may make a difference. If your aim is to do a team-building exercise, or to use humour, you must seat people close together. When an audience is spread out, each person feels more like an individual, and less like part of a crowd. A crowd laughs easily while isolated individuals do not. Seat people close together and, if they have already spread themselves throughout the auditorium, ask the MC to call them closer.

In a worst-case scenario, when an unforeseen interruption distracts your audience's attention, don't forge ahead. Stop and wait. You might make a quick joke about the interruption itself, but don't try to talk over it. Once the movement has stopped or the noise subsided, then and only then should you proceed.

Remember that you 'own' the time allotted for your presentation. Take charge of it in every sense, and make sure that the environment facilitates your message. After all, pianists insist on silence. Why shouldn't you?

---

**Quick tip!**
Get to know the stage beforehand, so that you will feel confident presenting from it. When no one else is in the room, walk around your speaking area, growing accustomed to the way the room looks and feels. You will give yourself a great advantage by performing this exercise. You will be less nervous if you are already familiar with your way around.

# 20 Ignore the cameras

So there you are, occupying your spot on stage in a large auditorium, spouting away and feeling the warmth of the audience's response, when suddenly you notice something beyond the glare of the lights: A camera! It's been trained on you all along, and you hadn't noticed.

You now wonder whether you should look at the audience or at the camera. Unsure, you switch from camera to audience and back to the camera again. Finally, you settle on looking directly into the lens and ignoring your audience entirely.

Or let's take a similar dilemma. You find yourself in a situation where photographers are constantly taking snapshots while you are speaking. What should you do? Speak directly to *them*? Or pause and pose for the snap?

Cameras do strange things to speakers. There is something about a camera that makes your speech feel somehow more 'real'. Prior to its arrival, you were just talking to a group of people. Once the camera flashes, your speech suddenly becomes more *official*. What's more, and of greater concern, is that there will now be a permanent record of your presentation, whereas before it was simply going to disappear into the ether.

What should you do? How should you react? Where should you direct your eyes?

The rule in dealing with cameras is exceptionally simple. Pretend that they aren't there. It really is that easy.

Should you be looking into the camera? The answer is 'no'. Just keep speaking to your audience. Should you change your performance in some way for the sake of a still photo? The answer remains 'no'. Go ahead as if the photographer wasn't there.

When you make eye contact with a camera, you quickly lose your audience. And the (diminished) audience reaction will be caught on film. Don't look into the lens. Don't react to the cameras in any way.

The analogy I like to use is that of a wedding video and the strange behaviour some guests display when they realise they are being filmed. They try to 'duck' in front of the camera, or smile and look the other way, or try to put their hand between themselves and the camera.

What they should do is take no notice of the camera. The only notable exception to this rule is if you are the presenter of a filmed documentary or, say, the TV news. But believe me, if you find yourself hosting a TV show, you will have been trained to deal with cameras.

As a mere public speaker, talking to a live audience, you should simply ignore any cameras. This applies even if your talk is being filmed for television. There is a big difference between having your speech filmed for TV, and actually presenting it on TV.

## 21 Manage your hand-outs wisely

Nine out of ten presenters who use hand-outs to supplement their talks make a fundamental mistake. They circulate the hand-outs either before or during their speeches. The results are as predictable as they are avoidable.

Distribute hand-outs at the beginning of your speech, and people will be reading them as you start to talk. Do it midway through your speech, and it will waste time as people ruffle through the paper and, once again, read instead of listening to you.

Keep your hand-outs till the end. You could even advise the audience not to bother taking notes as you will be providing the information later. But don't give your presentation away in advance.

Also, keep your hand-outs simple. They should list all the main points, and be clear and easy to follow. An effective hand-out might look something like this:

> You can
> # ESCAPE THE HAMSTER WHEEL!
> Become a productive thinker!
>
> *Hamsters make up rules that work against them*
>
> *Hamsters do things the way they've always been done*
>
> *Hamsters do what all other hamsters would do*
>
> ### Pest control for a more productive mind
>
> 1. Use your initiative
> 2. Be proactive and take chances
> 3. Stop asking, 'How should it be done?' Start asking, 'What do I want to achieve?'
> 4. Take ownership of your life
> 5. Use 'value-adds' for greater inroads
> 6. Think big
> 7. Develop inertia

Be careful not to use the handing-out process as your conclusion, though, because you will rob yourself of applause. You can either ask somebody else to hand the papers out for you or announce that they can be collected on the way out. Or, if you are selling any item such as a book at the end of your course, keep your hand-outs on a table at the back, and take the opportunity to chat and network with people informally when the hand-outs are picked up.

## Make sure *you* are the attraction, not your slide show  22

Remember our opening story about Thembi's bid? She had prepared 99 separate slides, with enough bullets to overthrow a small African country.

Contrary to a strange and enduring belief, people don't actually like watching lengthy slide shows. Not only that, but slides are not always the most effective way of conveying information.

We should resist the temptation to inflict PowerPoint displays upon people simply because we believe 'that's the way a presentation is done'. Ancient Greece was renowned for its great orators, men whose speeches have survived down the millennia, and they had no power outlets for their Proximas.

Can you remember a single PowerPoint presentation that you've watched? Would you consider it 'great', or in any way memorable? Quite often, slide shows are completely unnecessary, and can even detract from the effectiveness of a talk.

I once coached a speaker who does an excellent talk on mountain climbing. His great obstacle, though, was mastering the difference between a speech and a voice-over.

What he tended to do, in the early stages of his presentation, was to show breathtakingly beautiful slides of the ascent up the mountain, but instead of 'speaking' to us, he made the mistake of simply providing a voice-over narration to his slides: 'This is us at the base camp; this is us climbing the first hundred feet; this is us learning that yaks don't make great pets . . .', etc. He would stand immobile, facing his slides, not looking at the audience, keeping up this dreary, running commentary from beginning to end. Worse still, he didn't take a minute or two to establish a rapport with his audience before showing the first slide.

We managed to bring his talks to life by finally breaking his voice-over habit. He now begins his presentations by spending a couple of minutes getting to know the audience, and allowing them to become familiar and comfortable with him.

Thereafter, his new formula goes something like this: Bring up a new slide. Wait two seconds for the audience to take it in, and do their 'ooh-ing' and 'ah-ing'. Then turn to his listeners and use voice, gestures and enthusiasm to draw their attention back to himself. Tell them about that particular section of the climb, and 'act' out the incident that took place. Then, bring up the next slide, allow the audience a second or two to look at it, and repeat the process.

The difference was immediately noticeable. Before, his audience felt distanced from him, and although his talk was interesting, it was not at all engrossing. We were not able to 'feel' what he was going through. We were *receiving information*, rather than having a conversation – *getting the facts*, rather than living out his experiences.

So make sure you don't look at your own slides as you speak. If you do, you will have turned away from your audience. It's unnecessary. Simply bring up your slide, allow two seconds of silence while people take it in, and then draw them back into a 'conversation' with you. However spectacular they might be, your slides are not the show. They are merely an aid. *You* and your personality are the show.

### A quick guide to using PowerPoint
- Whenever possible, use visuals in slides rather than text.
- Keep special effects to a minimum. Yes, it's true that you can create a slide that dissolves into nothing, changes colour three times, and pulsates with flashing lights. But it will make your presentation look childish.
- Lines of text should ideally just appear on the screen (or at most, fade, fly in, or dissolve.) And if you are going to have things fly into the screen, make sure that they all fly in from the same side, and at the same speed, without accompanying sound effects. As usual, keep it simple.
- Where you must use text, choose key words over sentences or paragraphs. When you use entire sentences, people will read your slides rather than listen to you.
- Don't stand in the projector's light. A surprising number of presenters do this. And make sure the projector is not shining directly into your speaking area.

> - When using strong visuals, bring the slide up, allow two seconds of silence for the audience to take it in, then start speaking.
> - Conclude what you are saying about a particular slide before you bring up the next one. Have the confidence to pause while you change slides.
> - Face your audience and talk to them, Don't turn your back on them and address the slides.

## Speak to your audience 'where they are at'  23

I'd like you to meet Tannie Hestrie. She comes from a little dorp outside the city and is personal assistant to the head of the company. She works because she has to, not because she wants to. She is also a person sitting in the audience you are about to address.

Tannie Hestrie is a little bored with her job, but at least it pays the bills. Right now, as she sits in the audience waiting for you to begin, she is worrying about what to cook for dinner that night. She's also wondering whether she remembered to close the kitchen window this morning, because the cat might be stuck inside. She's quite looking forward to watching *Survivor* on TV.

This is Tannie Hestrie's world. And you are about to step into it.

The funny thing is that Tannie Hestrie will determine whether your speech is a success or not. If she doesn't laugh, there is no laughter. If she doesn't understand, your speech was not understood. If she doesn't clap her hands, there is no applause.

Were you planning on using an illustration that drew on skateboarding, loud music and extreme sports? What do you think Tannie Hestrie's reaction will be?

Audiences are made up of very different people – including people just like Tannie Hestrie. Some audiences are full of yuppies; others of more conservative oldies. An extreme-sport illustration might work very well for a high-school audience, but it's likely to leave Tannie Hestrie scratching her head in bewilderment.

This highlights the skill of learning to speak to people 'where they are at'. I came up against it when speaking internationally. As mentioned previously, I present an hour-long motivational talk entitled 'Escaping the Hamster Wheel'. The talk is about using your initiative, not thinking like a 'hamster'.

I was invited to do this presentation in Malawi. I only realised once I'd started speaking that most Malawians don't even keep pets, let alone something as unusual as a hamster. I had to explain what a hamster was, before my speech made any sense to them. It smacked of back-pedalling.

Conversely, I once spoke to a group of prisoners, deep within a medium-level security prison. From the outset, I understood there was a big potential divide between us, and I was determined to overcome it. So I asked myself, 'If I were a prisoner, and someone came to speak to me, what would I want him to do? What would I want him to *be*?' My answer changed the nature of the talk I delivered.

I decided that, placed in their situation, I would not want to be spoken at. I would be profoundly aware that this person had just stepped into my domain – a prison – as a free man, with a life and a career ahead. I would be watching for even the slightest hint of contempt on his part. I would be waiting to see if he spoke to me as a child, as a lesser person, or as a 'prisoner'. I would want to know if he cared about me. And so I changed my approach entirely. As the prisoners walked into the room, I made a point of shaking their hands, one by one. This caught them by surprise, and immediately reduced the distance between us. It helped to portray me as friendly and not aloof.

I dispensed with all formality, and started my speech with a smiling, 'Hi guys! I'm glad to be here.' I made a point of displaying, with my voice, facial expressions and body language that I *genuinely was* glad to be there, and spoke in a tone that suggested openness, honesty, with no hint of reserve or superiority.

As I went along, I asked questions, and allowed members

of the audience to answer. All along, I chatted with them as equals. When I wanted to make a point, or get a lesson across, I would speak about mistakes I'd made, and how I learnt from them.

The result was magical. They warmed to me and gave me a standing ovation at the end because I had spoken to them *where they were at*. Not physically or geographically, but psychologically.

Speak to your audiences *where they are at*. Try to understand what their needs are, what their daily lives are like, and what challenges they face. Then meet them there.

Your content may remain exactly the same for different audiences. I gave the same speech to the prisoners as I often do to companies. But your illustrations and level of spoken language will change markedly if you are conscious of where your audience is at. You wouldn't speak to a primary school audience the same way you would, for example, to a board of directors, would you?

Begin by asking the person who engaged you to speak about the nature and make-up of the audience. Are they young? Old? Educated? Labourers? Executives? Male? Female? Ethiopian?

Then, once you know a little about the audience, take the Tannie Hestrie test. Ask yourself whether your listeners will have a context for what you are saying. Will Tannie Hestrie in the third row actually *get it*? Will she enjoy it? Or is this not really for her? She is the source of my applause, and the reason I'm speaking. Her understanding is my objective, so I must speak to *her*.

# Keep your audience with you         24

Your speech started superbly. You broke the ice. You used humour and got the audience on your side. The momentum was there. The *energy* was thrilling. Everything was geared towards a successful presentation.

And then your 'getting-to-know-you' time ended and you went into speech mode. The audience could feel a tangible shift in energy levels and, in turn, they settled back into listening mode. The vibe in the room dropped, and it dropped at a particular and measurable time. It was at the point where you ended your fun 'introduction', and switched to the main body of the speech. Your voice suddenly changed and the dynamic altered.

Your listeners by now have gone into a passive state. Like a person sitting in front of TV, they have 'switched off'. They are merely watching, not getting truly involved.

Most speakers want to know how to keep an audience engaged over long periods. It's a valuable skill, and there are a number of ways of doing it.

Start by making sure there is no tangible 'break' in speaking style between your spontaneous opening section and the 'content-based' body of your speech. The first should flow into the second seamlessly, imperceptibly. It should never have an 'okay, now let's get serious' type of transition.

The difference lies in whether or not you are continuing to talk to the audience as in a good conversation, or whether you have switched into a drier 'presenting' mode.

Don't forget that the audience is always there, so you must work throughout on your relationship with them – not just in the opening section. You may even customise stories and examples to a particular group, or, midway through your presentation, make reference to someone with whom they are familiar. Do whatever it takes to avoid looking like you have lapsed into 'speech' mode. Your talk should sound like a conversation from beginning to end.

The ability to be entertaining is most important to your efforts to keep an audience on your side. But I'd like to focus on two other useful ways of keeping an audience with you that do *not* require you to be entertaining (but will nevertheless contribute towards an entertaining speech).

The first is to allow your audience enough time to digest each point, so that you don't lose them. The second is to ask questions.

As a speaker, we tend to rush through material. The reason for this is quite simple: we are familiar with it. We are halfway through a sentence, and already thinking about the next sentence, because the information is not new to us. We are also influenced by our nerves, and tend to 'rush' when we don't feel confident.

What you must remember is that your audience is hearing your presentation for the first time. To them, it is not as obvious as it is to you. The information is new, and at the end of every relevant point, they need a second or two to digest it. If they miss too many consecutive points, their attention will drift.

Here's what you can do. At the end of any line that
- makes a point,
- reaches the climax of a story,
- constitutes a punch line,
- concludes an explanation, or
- divulges information,

you should simply stop, and allow a few seconds for the audience to take in the information. A moment or two will do, and then you can proceed.

> **Quick tip!**
> If a point is particularly profound, pause for a longer period of time. The audience will perceive the importance of the point in relation to the length of time that you pause. A highly dramatic point might be left hanging in the air for up to ten seconds. Of course, pausing for that length of time takes courage. But it sounds superb!

The next thing is to continually ask questions. But why would you, as the presenter, ask your audience questions? Surely it should be the other way around?

Strangely enough, questions are a sign that you care about your audience. When you speak without asking questions for any length of time, you become in effect a 'lecturer', rather than a real person engaged in conversation with the audience. It's as if you have forgotten they were there, and would carry on regardless even if they all walked out of the room.

You can ask two kinds of questions: *rhetorical questions* that simply engage minds by inviting introspection, and *actual questions* to which you require an answer from the audience. You can use a healthy mix of both in your speeches, but rhetorical questions are often the more useful of the two.

Rhetorical questions give the impression of a conversation, without requiring the audience to answer out loud. A well-placed rhetorical question will receive a series of knowing nods and 'mm-hmms' from your audience. They simply help you to relate.

Let me show you what I mean. Here is a section of a speech, delivered without the use of rhetorical questions:

*Two days ago, I walked into a 7-Eleven shop where the lights were extremely bright. They hurt my eyes. It was late at night, and I felt grumpy. But when I walked up to the counter to purchase my items, the lady at the till was actually very friendly. I was surprised. It's not everyday you receive pleasant service. It made me feel extremely warm inside.*

Here is the same story, this time including rhetorical questions (admittedly overdoing it a little), for the purpose of continually engaging the audience and ensuring that they are relating to you:

*Two days ago, I walked into a 7-Eleven. Have you been into their stores? Have you seen how bright their lights are? They hurt my eyes. It was late at night, and I felt grumpy. You know what it's like when you've already climbed into bed, and only then did you realise there was no milk for breakfast? But when I walked up to the counter to purchase my items, the lady at the till was actually very friendly. I was surprised. Don't you find that pleasant service actually shocks you these days? It's not every day you receive it. It made me feel extremely warm inside – you know the feeling?*

The audience may listen to the first story, but they will smile and nod when hearing it told in the second manner. Questions re-engage the audience, and require them to stretch to meet you halfway. This is a valuable tool in your speaking kit.

Questions that require an answer can be just as good, but shouldn't be overused. Ask them in the same way as rhetorical questions, but pause and wait for an answer.

For example: 'I was recently down in Durban. Who here

comes from Durban? Three hands – thanks very much. Who's been there on holiday? Almost everyone! Good, thanks! Then you'll probably be familiar with this charming little restaurant on the beachfront . . .'

# Speak with vibrancy 25

Because your voice is such a critical element of a speech, we'll dedicate a fair amount of attention to it.

I once met a brilliant young South African living in Germany. Mark is a doctor, conducting cancer research in Berlin. He is bright, obviously, and his thoughts and theories are fascinating. But Mark has a problem of which he isn't even aware. He speaks in a monotone. Not in a low, sensuous voice that varies a little here and there, but in a flat, mind-numbing mumble.

Mark is constantly complaining that he doesn't have a girlfriend – which is strange, given his relative wealth, reasonable looks and exceptional intelligence. But he is not even vaguely aware that people's toes start to curl by the time he is halfway through one of his monologues.

If a monotone is unpleasant in a social setting, it's much worse in an hour-long speech. The audience goes to sleep.

On the other hand, a lilting, energised and pleasant voice, with plenty of vocal variety, can cause an audience to 'lean in', listen more closely, and even become carried away. I have an elderly Irish friend, to whom I can listen to for hours on end, simply to take in the cadence of those lilting Celtic tones. He could read out of the phone-book for all I care. He has that sort of voice.

Have you ever heard yourself speak? If your career involves a lot of public speaking, then it's worth your while investing some time (and possibly money) in finding out how you sound to an audience.

Use a video recorder, or a handheld digital audio recorder of the type that journalists use. Or simply record a cellphone

greeting with your service provider, and then play it back to yourself. As you listen to your own voice, ask yourself:
- Does my pitch vary up and down? (It should)
- Do I mumble, or am I unclear? (You shouldn't be)
- Do I pronounce my syllables clearly? (You must)

If you've answered these questions honestly and discovered that you have work to do, here is a simple exercise that can help. Try reading aloud out of a book. Choose a novel, because it will have greater dramatic potential, which means more opportunity to use inflection and range, and work on the particular aspect of your voice that needs correction. It may be tedious to have to listen to yourself, but why then should you expect your audience to do so? Take a deep breath, and start to practise using your voice more effectively.

Be careful, always, of building up the level of tension in your voice and holding on to it for long periods. Your audience will think you are screaming at them. Come down in pitch from time to time, and then rebuild to your next peak. Keep varying your tone, pace, volume and rhythm. Pause and break rhythm, and start to build it up again.

Your voice has the potential to charm if you are prepared to use it properly.

Take care, also, not to sound 'speechy'. That often happens to people who are not accustomed to public speaking. They believe their voice should have a nasal, sing-song quality, their phrases should be formal, lengthy, and they should draw heavily on clichés such as 'It is therefore my pleasure to ...', and, 'In conclusion, ladies and gentlemen', and other overused phrases.

The last thing a speech should sound like is a speech. A stage play only sounds like a play when it is performed by amateurs. If it's done properly, by skilled actors, you will forget you are watching a production that was originally written on paper and rehearsed for hours. You will forget you are hearing lines from a script. Instead, you will simply become immersed in the moment, absorbed by the magic of a great story. You will believe – just for a moment – that you are watching real people going through an ordeal before your own eyes.

The drama will not seem staged. Properly done, it will simply look like *life!*

Speaking is the same. Your aim is not to sound like 'a speaker', but just the opposite. You should try to sound perfectly natural, as though you were having a friendly conversation with a single person. Your audience should be able to forget that your words were once a script, and feel that you are 'talking' to them — naturally and sincerely.

So drop the notion of a sing-song, 'official' speaking voice and talk conversationally. Like an actor, you need to know your content so well that it ceases to sound scripted and more like normal speech, accompanied by all the facial expressions, gestures and enthusiasm that you would bring to an enthusiastic chat. If you know the content of your speech thoroughly, you should be able to do this easily.

> **Quick tip!**
> Would you like to sound a little classier? Less homespun South African? Start with the way you pronounce the 'i' sound. We typically pronounce it on a lower, more guttural level. A sentence such as: 'This is it, the place where we swim,' will sound something like, 'Thus uhs uht. thuh place where we swuhm,' in South African.
>
> Also, beware also of dropping the word 'are'. so that a sentence like 'We are going to the shops,' becomes, 'We going to the shops.'
>
> With enough conscientious practice, you can improve the way you sound. Just don't overcorrect. or your friends and family will have a good, hearty South African laugh at you!

# Control nervous tics and twitches 26

One of my students had a habit of 'bouncing' as he spoke. He would continually lift himself onto his toes, and then lower himself again. He wasn't even aware that he did it — until we put him in front of a mirror. Then he was horrified.

Any form of repetitive movement is visually distracting. You can see it from a mile away, believe me. You may think that fiddling with your jacket as you speak, because you're a little nervous, isn't really noticeable, but unfortunately, it jumps out at an audience. It's like a lighthouse in the night, visible from miles around.

Do you remember those TV ads about skin cream for teenagers? They would depict a young man trying to flirt with a girl but feeling self-conscious because of the spinning light on his forehead (representing the dreaded pimple). That's what physical tics are like to your audience. They are beacons, and they draw the eye.

Here are a few of the more popular ones:

- **The ticking clock** – in which a speaker sways pendulously left to right. A few minutes of this can actually hypnotise an audience.
- **The hillbilly two-step** – similar to the ticking clock, only more pronounced. Instead of swaying from one side to the other, the speaker actually steps to the left, then steps to the right ('Yee-ha! Grab your partner, dozy-do!').
- **Restless hands** – a dead giveaway of nervousness, and a predominantly male trait. Men tend to massage the flesh on the inside of their palms, while women fiddle with their hands at their sides, either crumpling up the bottom corners of their jackets or 'ironing' the slacks they are wearing.
- **The forehead swoop** – characteristic of (but not limited to) women. A constant, repetitive brushing aside of the fringe.
- **The gyrating schoolgirl** – Imagine a little girl of five or six who is shy, but is being forced to talk to someone. She keeps her feet firmly on the ground, but gyrates at the hips, as she turns her face from left to right. Often encountered in the corporate world.
- **The nervous cough** – when the speaker constantly clears his or her throat or coughs dryly at the end of every second sentence.
- **Check the chin** – Occasionally you may see speakers checking, with a quick rub of the hands, to see if their

chin is still there. The nose is a popular alternative. Yet rubbing your nose every few seconds makes it look as though you are essentially untrustworthy – if not a liar.

Practise speaking in front of a mirror in private. Keep going for a few minutes and see if you can pick up what nervous habits you have. Or watch yourself on video. You should recognise your bad habits right away, and take steps to correct them.

Habits are completely breakable. I know, because I had a few quirks when I began speaking, and as a result of conscious effort, I've overcome them. It wasn't particularly hard to do. But you must first become aware of what you do.

# Be wary of crutch words 27

We use many verbal crutches in normal speech. Prime examples include: 'Like', 'Actually', 'Kind of', and of course the perennial and much-loved 'Okay'.

These words are stopgaps while we try to, like, kind of, think of our next sentence, you know. The problem is, once we start to lean on these crutch words, it becomes difficult to stop using them. We repeat them over and over again. And the audience is quick to notice it.

My own verbal crutch, while learning the ropes of radio broadcasting, was 'Great!'

I once received a phone call, off air, from a listener who took me to task. 'I really enjoy your show,' he said. 'And I tune in often. But if you say the word 'great' one more time, I'm switching stations!'

The danger with verbal crutches is that your audience stops listening to your content, and starts concentrating on the word. I once counted 35 uses of the word 'actually' in a seven-minute long presentation. If your listeners have become aware of an annoying verbal glitch, they're no longer hearing your arguments.

There is a two-part solution to the problem. Part one is becoming aware of it. You will only realise the damage a tic is doing to your presentation when you hear it for yourself. While you are speaking, you will not even be aware you're doing it. So record yourself on audiotape or videotape and listen for verbal crutches. You will then be halfway to solving the problem.

Part two is to remind yourself of your habit during your presentation. Once you've identified your verbal crutch, ask a friend in the audience to count the number of times you lean on it. Generally, the awareness that someone in the audience is monitoring you will be sufficient to make you avoid using the offending word.

Confidence in your material plays a large role here too. I find that when I'm less than prepared for a particular segment on talk-radio, my crutch words become more pronounced. I struggle more as I try to buy time to think. The better prepared I am, the less my mind relies on this back-pedalling technique.

Another kind of verbal crutch to be avoided is the dreaded 'um'. Why do we say 'um' so much when we speak? We obviously don't intend to. It, um, somehow sort of just happens. But why?

We use 'um' whenever we are unsure of our content, or are trying to figure out what to say next. The way to stop is no different from the solution suggested for other verbal crutches. Be aware of your 'ums' and make a conscious effort to reduce them. Record yourself and listen to the recording. Ask a friend or audience member to count the number of times you say 'um'. Rehearse your speech, and get to know your content to the point where you no longer need to resort to verbal crutches.

Finally, take a pause whenever you stop to think. Fill any gaps with silences, not with 'ums'. Pauses are thinking spaces and the greatest favour you can do yourself is to pause frequently. If you want to be really hard on yourself (and I would only recommend this for the thick-skinned), you could ask a friend to listen to your talk and to tap on a glass each time you say 'um'. Instant feedback is a highly effective teacher!

## Rehearse your speech while writing it    28

Why would you need to rehearse a speech before delivering it? Surely it's just a collection of sentences which, once written and memorised, can simply be spoken out loud? Write it first, then speak it. Right?

If that were the case, all speakers would be roughly equal in ability. And clearly this is not the case. There are some who are orators and others so painful to listen to that we make an excuse to leave the room.

Rehearsing makes the biggest difference. A speech may look fine on paper, but its delivery in front of a live audience is what really counts. Both Adolf Hitler and Winston Churchill, each known for their great oratorical powers, would practise their speeches for hours on end. If these master orators believed in extensive rehearsal, then so should we.

These are some of the problems caused by *not* rehearsing a speech:

- Your thoughts will not be as clear or structured as they could be.
- Because you've never spoken it out loud, your language sounds like 'written' rather than 'spoken' English. If you've done no rehearsing, you will only discover this in front of your audience – when it's too late.
- Because you haven't practised telling your stories, you may stumble over them and leave out important details. It's embarrassing to get two-thirds of the way through a story and then say something like, 'Oh, but what I forgot to tell you was . . .'
- Humour requires more rehearsing than anything else. You must know your punch line, and be able to deliver it with confidence and timing.

Ideally, begin to rehearse your speech while you're busy writing it. In other words, read it aloud as you complete the writing of each paragraph. Your ear will quickly pick up whether what you have written sounds 'natural' or not. We tend to write longer sentences than are necessary in a speech, with the result that we either run out of breath in the delivery or sound stilted.

Shorter, 'chattier' sentences and informal language work much better than their antitheses. (Take the word 'antitheses' as an example – in a speech you would simply say 'opposites'.)

Once the speech is written, do a dry run in a quiet room. Don't practise it in front of your PC – you need to become familiar with delivering the words standing up, the way you actually do live. If you are able to use a mirror, so much the better. A full-length mirror is ideal, but any large mirror will do. Begin by delivering sections of your speech, without looking at your notes. Your goal is to become familiar with 'how' your words will come out. Once you've done that, deliver the complete speech from beginning to end.

Don't worry too much if you have to look at your notes occasionally while rehearsing. But aim to deliver progressively longer sections without notes. This will help you grow accustomed to 'telling' each story and explaining each thought.

For truly important presentations, don't hesitate to get a friend or trusted mentor to listen as you rehearse your speech. Speaking in front of another person for the first time causes you to focus properly, to clarify your thoughts and to express yourself exactly. It quickly exposes flaws too.

Another prime time for speech rehearsal is when you find yourself sitting in traffic. Turn your radio down, and deliver your presentation aloud. It's very important to do it *out loud*, so that you can hear your own voice delivering the speech.

True, other motorists might take you for a nutter, but don't worry about them. Speaking aloud helps you to fix the content of the speech in your mind.

> **Quick tip!**
> Do you value your sleep? Then you'll find it's better not to think about your speech as you lie in bed at night. While this may seem like a perfect time to practise, you'll soon discover that a combination of mental stimulation and nerves will prevent you from switching off and getting to sleep. Thinking your way through a speech has a highly stimulating effect on your mind. So use with caution!

# Appeal to the imagination    29

Why invoke the human imagination when you're giving a business presentation that requires a degree of formality? Won't alluding to the imagination reduce your credibility?

This is a common but an ill-founded view. Every audience is made up of people who share a number of basic traits – fear, anger, joy, sorrow, excitement, disgust, jealousy, desire, etc. – no matter what their age or level of education.

To some extent, we all need to have our emotions stirred. And the access point is the imagination. Gerry Spence, one of America's most famous trial lawyers, wrote a book titled *How to Argue and Win Every Time*, in which he went to great pains to illustrate that every truly effective speech starts in what he terms 'the heart zone' and ultimately appeals to the imagination. His impressive track record is the result of learning how to speak to 'ordinary people'.

The assumption that formality is more effective than appeals to the imagination is completely unfounded. Over the years, I've listened to a great many talks by CEOs, upper and middle-level managers, sales people and the like, and without fail, the best presentations were those that appealed to the imagination. The dignity and decorum were there, but so was the magic.

Not long ago, I heard the then CEO of Anglo American, Lazarus Zim, deliver a high-level talk that contained a lot of imaginative storytelling. And he charmed his audience. Imagination and seriousness are never mutually exclusive in the speaking trade.

Let's look at some examples of presentations typically perceived as 'dry' that could be brought to life by use of the imagination:

- A talk on architecture: Describe what the view is like from the top of the building you are talking about, speak about the kind of lifestyle a family could enjoy in the space provided, depict the pain and struggle that early stonemasons went through in the construction of a similar

building, or the amount of money that the project could have cost had a different technique been used.
- An explanation of how a financial product works: List, for example, the advantages the product could bring to a real family, or describe how one spouse suffered from the other's failure to take out life insurance.
- A sales pitch: Paint pictures of the discomfort of a world without your product, Tell us about the exciting vista that will open once your product has been purchased. Make your audience see it, feel it, *taste* it!

Even the driest topic affords some opportunity to cater to the imagination. Don't forget that the imaginative, creative part of the mind constitutes an entire side of one's brain.

So how do you inject the imagination into your talk?
1. Tell stories.
   This is your greatest ally in communication, and we will go into more detail about it in the next section.
2. Involve the audience in your illustrations.
   In one of my motivational talks, I use a very simple technique to illustrate a point. I ask for a volunteer to come forward from the audience. I walk her to one side of the stage, and place a tennis ball in her hand. I kneel down and place a line of tape on the ground directly before her feet. Then I walk to the far side of the stage, where I put a small glass cup on the floor. Only then do I explain what I want her to do, 'Your mission is to get the ball into the cup. Three ... two ... one ... go!'
   Without fail, my volunteer will try to throw the ball into the glass from behind the tape. Of course, this is impossible. Even in the rare event that his or her aim is good enough to hit the rim of the cup, the latter will simply fall over from the force of the ball.
   I allow a number of volunteers to try their hand, until the inevitable moment when a light bulb goes on and someone realises that one can simply walk over to the glass and place the ball directly into it. Of course, I had never specified that anybody had to stand behind the tape. The

rule was merely implied. In the context of my talk, this was to illustrate the way in which we *make up rules that work against us*.

I could have gone the route of simply explaining, 'Sometimes we make up rules and limitations that get in our own way, and we shouldn't.' But how effective do you think that would have been in comparison? I chose instead to *show* it to them, to involve them in the process, and create a metaphor they will not forget. Everyone has a good laugh, and because their imaginations were engaged, they are likely to remember the point I was making afterwards.

3. Use interesting metaphors and icons.

The title of one of my set talks, 'Escape the Hamster Wheel', is a metaphor. The talk is about learning to use your own initiative, thinking creatively, and taking charge of your own life. But imagine if I had titled it, 'Learning to use your own initiative, thinking creatively, and taking charge of your own life . . .' Not nearly as snappy, is it?

I continually use the metaphor of 'corporate hamsters', people who run endlessly on their little running wheels, never truly getting anywhere, never stopping to ask *why?*. Symbols and icons of this kind cement ideas in the minds of your audiences. Be creative and use them well.

4. Appeal to the senses.

If you truly want to engage an audience's attention, appeal to their *senses*. Don't just say that a building was 'very tall'. Describe its spires 'piercing through wisps of white cloud', talk about how the viewing deck makes you dizzy as you stare out at the sprawling city miles below, or how you might hurt your neck if you stood at its base and tried to look up at the top.

Don't just relate facts like a journalist; paint pictures like an artist. Sights, sounds, smells, colour, movement, textures and emotions – these are your tools. Bring them all into your speech.

The truly daring may even venture (carefully) into the realm of the semi-erotic. Few things engage the imagination as quickly as the sensual. Of course, as with all instances in which you play with fire, use this technique with extreme caution, and only if you are quite certain that your audience will appreciate it.

5. Appeal to the emotions.
Stir the emotions and you will create empathy. We all feel fear, anger, joy, sorrow, excitement, disgust and jealousy. Everyone understands weariness, ambition, desire and disappointment. Import some of these emotions into your speech and you will create an empathy with your audience.

It might be the difference between: 'I created this company from scratch, as a poor kid from a rundown neighbourhood . . .'

And, 'I'll never forget how I used to burn with jealousy when I watched wealthy people drive past our dirty street, as they hurried off to the gleaming buildings downtown. I'd sit on the pavement and dream about "someday". That stirred my desire to get out, to grow, to learn, to live. And it was a desire that would not be satisfied until the day I gazed out from my penthouse on the top floor of this spectacular building . . .'

Can you see the difference? More pertinently, can you *feel* it? The first example merely relates facts – the second *takes you there!*

Stir emotions to create empathy. Invite people to dream dreams, and play on basic human traits.

6. Use humour.
Laughter is a refreshing release in the middle of a complex argument or a long presentation. Don't be afraid to use it. However, don't rely too heavily on simply telling jokes. Especially old ones. The best humour is often nothing more than a few 'throwaway' lines.

I'll give you an example. A Zulu lady, who missed her calling to be a praise singer, once introduced me to an audience. At the top of her voice, she yelled that I was 'The world's greatest speaker! An amazing man! This genius who will uplift us and change our very lives forever . . .'etc., etc. She went so far over the top she had the audience giggling at her.

I walked to the front of the room, wide-eyed, and simply said, 'Wow!' That single word, showing my embarrassment and amazement at the introduction, almost brought the house down. It also made me look a little more humble than I would have looked had I simply begun talking, implying that I endorsed every word she had said.

My next line was a throwaway, 'You're hired!' It wasn't a proper joke and didn't require a lot of telling. But it worked.

I carried on, 'I'm not sure what for, but you're hired!' (Another throwaway line – more laughter.) 'In fact, would you like to get married?' (Third throwaway – even more laughter.) 'You know I've always wanted my own professional praise singer.' (Fourth throwaway.) 'I feel like a politician!' (Fifth throwaway.)

Do you see how easy it is? I said all of this in a friendly, smiling manner, so that it wouldn't come across as though I was teasing her. It worked like a charm, because a good throwaway line is often better than a hackneyed joke you may have read on e-mail or heard at a pub. This is not to say that telling jokes is out of the question, provided you find one that is relevant to the day and to your content. But one-liners are by far the best kind of humour in a speech. Stand-up comedy, after all, is little more than a series of consecutive one-liners, generally developed around a theme.

# Turn your points into stories 30

Nothing affords a better opportunity to invoke the imagination than storytelling. I once heard a phrase that stuck in my mind: 'Stories are the medium of human communication.'

Religious texts such as the Bible make extensive use of stories, and Jesus' lessons were all delivered as parables (illustrative stories). Two thousand years later, their messages live on.

A speech that makes no use of the most basic example or

illustration lacks an 'anchor' for its message. It's a collection of words with no substance. If the audience is going to listen to you for any length of time, you need to give them meat.

Another advantage of storytelling is that it can be very economical. Stories summarise complex points swiftly and easily. Professional speakers often meet past members of an audience, who say something like, 'I still remember that story you told about dropping yoghurt on your wife's new carpet, and her reaction . . . !'

They will never say, 'I remember the point you made about owning up to mistakes at home.' No, they remember the story you told. And if they remember the story, they got the point.

You may have noticed that almost every section in this book tells a story, or gives an example. My intention is to break the monotony of reading 'dry' advice, and provide you with real, 'appeal-to-the-imagination' tales of what works and what doesn't. I employ this technique equally in my writing and speaking.

So:

- Tell a story first, and make the point afterwards. The story will clarify the idea in your audience's mind, and provide an 'anchor' from which to make your point.
- Take to heart the maxim of every good writer: 'Don't tell – show!' Don't summarise an incident – paint the picture.
- Finding stories is not as difficult as it may seem. You can draw on small, amusing incidents from home or work – just the ordinary stuff of life.

In order to make a point about people having different goals in life, a speaker I heard told a story that essentially went like this: 'One morning, while my wife and I were travelling abroad, I awoke early on the 18th floor of the hotel. I'm a morning person, but my wife isn't. I wanted her to come and look at the beautiful sunrise from the balcony, but she had asked me to let her sleep in. Still, it was so beautiful that I thought I'd awaken her anyway. So I pulled the blankets off the bed, grabbed her by the leg, and said, "Honey, come and look at this right now!" . . . And you know what? She said something that hurt my feelings . . . !'

This simple story had the audience in stitches! It was nothing special, but it illustrated beautifully the point about two people having differing goals, and made a perfect starting point for his presentation.

- Your stories need not be complicated; they need only be amusing or entertaining, or tug a little at the heartstrings.
- Start to collect 'stock' stories in a file. You can recycle anecdotes you've read somewhere, but tales told in the first person, i.e. your own experiences, are always better.

I often relate the story of my first day presenting on radio, and the chaos surrounding my first show. I can make a myriad of points with that story – everything from communications training, to day jobs in general, or advice on career planning. You should start to collect stories of your own, and use them in your presentations.

- All stories need a few basic ingredients. They must have conflict, and a resolution to that conflict. 'Conflict' could be something as simple as the cross-purposes in the story about the man and wife in a hotel, with him wanting her to see the sunrise, and her wanting to sleep in. Resolution would simply be the outcome of that conflict (which, in his case, was probably no TLC for a month!)

# Use 'we' instead of 'you' 31

'Let's talk about your kind of person. I know what you people are like! You're all the same, aren't you?'

How does the above phrase strike you? Did it leave you feeling warm? Or did it sound unfriendly, even hostile?

Surprisingly, a great number of speakers use phrases like this all the time – perhaps not as overtly as in the example above – and immediately distance themselves from their audience.

The simplest of phrases can make you an 'outsider' in an audience's eyes. It can also mean the difference between coming across as a caring person or a distant, authoritative figure.

When saying anything prescriptive, controversial, or even vaguely admonishing, use the term 'we', and not 'you'.

Let me show you what I mean. Here is the wrong way to phrase such a thought: 'You South Africans can be very racist. You need to change that.'

The same thought would be much more acceptable, and much less of an accusation, if you simply said, 'We South Africans can be very racist. We need to change that.'

In the second instance, you become 'part' of the audience. You take accountability alongside them. Instead of pointing fingers at others, you give the impression of sharing the blame yourself.

Beware of segregationist language that separates you from your audience. The idea, at all times, is to relate to your listeners and elicit empathy. How can you expect empathy when you are accusing your audience of something unpleasant?

The same applies in other instances. A phrase like, 'You guys must meet target this month' is infinitely improved by saying, 'We must meet our targets this month.'

Make sure you are playing on the same team as your audience. If not, don't be surprised when they won't call you 'coach.'

## 32 Speak as if to a single person

After my first few shows on radio, an experienced member of the senior staff, himself an old hand at presenting, took me aside in a corridor and asked, 'When you address listeners, who are you speaking to?'

Luckily, I'd received a significant amount of training in public speaking by then, and gave the answer quickly: 'One person,' I said.

'That's exactly right!' he replied.

When you talk to an audience, it's tempting to use phrases like 'All of you', 'Everybody', or, 'Each member of this audience here today'. These words are unnecessary and actually distance us from the people we are speaking to.

I've said many times that our goal is to sound like we're having a 'conversation' with our audience. The second we address them in the plural, we damage the illusion of a conversation.

Have you ever heard a person say, 'I felt as though she was speaking directly to me!' If so, it's a sign that the speaker knew his or her stuff. And it's simple enough to do.

Use the singular, not the plural where possible. Instead of using phrases like 'You guys', or 'Everyone here today', address the crowd as though you were speaking to just one person: 'Have you ever been in a situation like that?', 'How did you feel?', 'I'd like you to join me in a toast . . .' etc.

Speaking in the singular sounds more intimate and familiar, and builds rapport more readily. Next time you happen to be listening to your favourite radio presenter, pay attention to the way in which he or she addresses you, the listener. You will quickly discover that the best broadcasters have been trained to speak to you in the singular.

# Avoid paralanguage    33

Aha! Paralanguage – the bugbear of the mid-level manager! What, I hear you ask, is paralanguage? Allow me to illustrate:

This is how a simple, ten-second section from a corporate presentation might sound:

'Thanks very much for being here. I'm thrilled to announce the arrival of our new product. It has many applications for your clients. Let's take a look at some of them. First off, we can use it at home to clean the pool . . .'

This is the same piece, with the addition of paralanguage:

'Thanks very much for being here. I know you're all very busy. Well, I mean some of you are busy, and others aren't. There are deadlines in the marketing department.

'But anyway . . . I'm thrilled to announce the arrival of our new product. Actually, it arrived yesterday. Well, not the product, but the packaging, just so that we can see what the product is like. Okay, back to what I was saying. The product has many applications for your clients. Some of your customers like having more uses. I know Jenni said something about that to me last week. What was it you said, Jenni? Well, it wasn't important. But let's take a look at some of the applications. First off – and when I say "first", I don't mean that this is the most important one. Well, I guess it could be to some of you. But first off, we could use it at home to clean the pool . . . I suppose not everyone has a pool. But that doesn't matter. Anyway . . .'

Painful, isn't it? Yet I bet you know someone who does it. Paralanguage dilutes thought and clogs ideas. And besides, it makes the speaker look indecisive, which is the last quality a manager should wish to display.

Some of the offending phrases include 'Anyway', 'But that's another story', 'I'll tell you about that later' and 'Actually, what I meant was . . .'

I once watched a speaker show a video clip of a sporting hero and say, 'Here he is, breaking the world record!' We all sat up to watch. Then, with our curiosity and sense of expectation heightened, he paused for a second and added, 'Well, actually, this isn't him. It's just an actor.' It was completely unnecessary.

Speak straightforwardly and don't undermine your own points with little asides. Don't feel the need to justify every word. The more you saturate your speech with paralanguage, the more you dilute the potency of your points, and the less authoritative you will sound.

# 34 Deliver emotion tactfully

I am a big believer in using *The Three H's* when constructing a speech: *Head, Heart* and *Humour.* Writing with this formula in mind ensures that you appeal in turn to your audience's:

- heads, via logic and reasoning,
- hearts, through the use of emotion, and
- sense of humour.

However, I would like to issue a strong word of caution about telling emotional stories. The 'bloodbath' formula – where one overdoses on sorrow and tragedy – was popular twenty years ago, but is now considered unacceptable.

Funnily enough though, an overemotional speech has less to do with content than with the manner of delivery. You can certainly get away with telling highly emotional stories, full of tears and trauma, but it must be done properly if it is to be acceptable. There is a right and wrong way of going about it.

Let's take, as an example, a story about a terrible, unnatural death. The content of such a story is inherently moving so you don't need to overdramatise it. If you do, your audience will feel manipulated. Just tell the story gently, tenderly, the way you would tell it to another person over a cup of coffee, showing consideration for the deceased and family. Be polite, soft-voiced and speak with genuine concern. It's the difference between telling us about how someone you loved passed away, and how 'this guy was blown to pieces!'

If told sincerely, your story will move people. It will sound more 'real'. And the audience will not feel manipulated.

The simple lesson is: don't overdo it. Just explain calmly what happened. It will be much more effective, and your audience will appreciate your not overstepping the mark.

## Use pauses consciously and often    35

I am a great advocate of the *pause*. In fact, if I'm ever asked what the single most effective speaking technique is, I unhesitatingly answer: '*Pausing*.'

What do I mean by pausing? The concept is not difficult. It means speaking, stopping, and then speaking again.

You do not have to be a rocket scientist to do it.

But here's the catch: using pauses in front of a live audience is profoundly difficult. It requires extreme confidence. Why? Because you are required to stop speaking, stare into a sea of eyes, all of which are staring back at you, and do no more than stand there. The pressure to quickly continue speaking is almost unbearable and it takes a seasoned speaker to resist rushing on.

Just to clarify, I'm not referring to those awkward moments of silence when a speaker forgets his or her next words. The type of pauses I'm referring to are those used for dramatic emphasis. They can be employed in a number of different ways.

Begin by determining consciously to use pauses, right from the start of your presentation. If you are unaccustomed to using them, write them into the script. After speaking in public often, you will develop a sense of which specific lines are important enough to warrant a good pause.

Build up your pace, pitch and volume as you deliver a key sentence. Then stop, and hold eye contact with your audience. You may even indulge in a 'knowing' look around the room, depending on the point you're trying to make. When a few moments of silence have elapsed, launch into your next line.

Here are a few examples of sentences that might merit a pause, showing where you might place these pauses:

'Our turnover will be double what it is today!' (Pause for effect.)

'But there is a new terror on the horizon...' (pause – build anticipation) 'A nameless terror!'

'There are three things you need to know' (pause – create expectation). 'The first is this...' (Pause.)

'Do you have any idea how much that is? It's like taking three US battleships and packing them full of money!' (Pause for the audience to digest a reference to 'size' or 'amount'.)

'Will you take up the challenge?' (Hypothetical question – pause for the audience to think about it).

'...And that's when I reached out, turned the chair around and discovered who it was (pause). All along, it had been none other than my own father!' (Climax of story – pause.)

The longer your pause, the more profound your point will seem. If you really want the audience to take in something important, take a longer pause.

You can even use pauses mid-sentence if you want to emphasise a specific word. Let's say that your sentence is, 'There is only one way I can convince you of that.' The important word in this sentence is 'convince'. You might deliver the sentence like this, 'There is only one way I can . . . convince you . . . of that.'

Pauses have the additional benefit of allowing you time to think, and to construct your next sentence. You won't make it through an hour-long talk easily without regular pauses.

Not only that, but good pauses make you look masterful. People who are truly confident will take their time, and their relaxed state gives them an air of authority.

Contrarily, nervous speakers always rush their thoughts, as if to get their talk over quickly. They speak as if apologising for being there, and their breathing is shallow and rapid. The irony is that the more they rush, the less they breathe, and the worse their anxiety becomes.

So use pauses confidently, liberally, and strategically. They will both enhance your speech and give you, the speaker, more time to think.

# Don't hide behind notes 36

Do you always use cue cards? You don't have to. In fact, cards can actually get in your way. I hope I can persuade you to stop using them entirely.

There are advantages and disadvantages to using cue cards.

The advantages are:
1. You won't need to memorise difficult statistics, names or quotations.

2. You have an outline in front of you, should you forget where you are in your speech.

The disadvantages are:
1. You will almost inevitably end up sounding as if you are reading, which may detract from your speech.
2. You lose eye contact with your audience, as you constantly look down at the cards.
3. If you do lose your place, or if you should drop them, cue cards can actually be counterproductive. Instead of just moving on, you will be tempted to stand there reading through them, trying to find your line.
4. It makes your speech sound like a 'speech'. Cue cards suggest you are 'going through the motions', rather than 'connecting with us'. I am all for speaking without cue cards. Make eye contact with your audience, and speak directly to them, with warmth and charm.

However, if you feel you must go the cue card route, here are some pointers:
1. Never have more than four or five cards — maximum.
2. Number each of the cards, in the same place on each card, so you need not shuffle through them trying to find your place.
3. Never write out sentences or paragraphs. Ever! Just write keywords. When you write out sentences, you will inevitably end up hiding behind your notes and reading to the audience. Your cue cards are only there as quick references, so that you can glance down at them, look back up and continue speaking.

Better than cue cards are simple drawings, in the tradition of mind maps. Rather than write a reminder such as 'Sales team to buy in', draw a little doodle of a salesman smiling and handing over money. Your mind will take this in far quicker than it can read a line in a paragraph, which means you'll be able to simply glance down, then look straight back up again, confident of your next point.

# Use an essay style rather than lists

## 37

In the world of video-making and video-editing, there is a standing rule: *Never list.* This means that when making a video about a product, for example, you should never merely list one benefit after the other. Your voice-over would sound something like this, 'And it can do this, and it can do this, and it can do this, and ...'

Instead, the seasoned producer will break up each thought, and deliver it creatively, in documentary style.

The same applies to speeches. It's all too easy to revert to *list* mode: *this, and this, and this, and* ... It often crops up in wedding speeches: 'And I'd like thank Joan, and Sandra, and George ...'

Listing sets off a dull-sounding rhythm, and gives the audience the cue to lull off. It says, 'This section isn't important – we're running through the formalities.'

When writing your speech, think more in terms of an essay than a list. Remember what would happen if you turned in a list as your English paper? Do it to an audience, and they will groan just as loudly as your Grade 7 teacher used to do.

Delete all phrases that hint at a list, such as, 'And then I'd like to thank ...' and 'It can also ...'

To clarify, let me give you an example. In a wedding speech, in which a number of people must be thanked, this is how it would sound using the listing technique.

'And I'd like to thank Tannie Marie for baking such a wonderful cake, and Steve for loaning us his gleaming Mercedes-Benz for the bridal couple's use, and I'd also like to thank Jannie for this venue. It's really beautiful, Jannie! And I'd like to thank Chris and Penny for driving all this way. And I'd also like to thank the bridesmaids. Don't they look lovely today?'

By being a little creative, you can avoid the dreary repetition of a list:

'Tannie Marie baked the cake you see in the middle of the floor. Tannie, you are an angel, and we are grateful for the time you spent creating this masterpiece. Steve made a great personal sacrifice too, by providing his gleaming Mercedes Benz for the bridal couple's use. Well done, Steve! Jannie, this venue is beautiful! And it was exceptionally considerate of you to offer it without even being asked. We are here today as a result of your generosity, and the ambience is everything we'd hoped for. Chris and Penny drove a great distance to be here, for which the bridal couple are extremely grateful. It wouldn't have been the same without you guys! And don't the bridesmaids look lovely today?'

Notice how much more natural the speech sounds? And it draws the audience in, rather than switching them off by going into a rhythm that says, 'here comes a list'.

## 38 Always walk your talk

A friend relates the story of how he was working for a large bank in Johannesburg, when a group of consultants were called in for a day-long seminar on *image management*.

(I usually enjoy these seminars. There is always something new and fascinating to learn about the way dress, look, posture, speech and body language reveal different aspects of one's personality.)

This group of trainers did something strange, though. They arrived at the bank in casual clothes – jeans, sneakers and T-shirts. One of the ladies was pregnant, and had chosen to wear a tight little vest, without a jacket, that highlighted her growing belly and displayed her pronounced cleavage.

This made the delegates feel particularly uncomfortable. (Perhaps some of the guys approved – who knows?) Not only that, the trainers were directly contradicting their own message about dressing for authority in the workplace. They looked as if they were dressed for a lazy Sunday afternoon at home. By their own measure, they were showing disrespect for their client.

I always wonder about this particular incident. It seems such a bizarre oversight that I was tempted to leave it out of the book in case you think it contrived. But it really happened.

No one said anything in front of the trainers. The bank's employees were too polite to point out the contradiction between theory and practice. But HR was quietly advised never to hire them again. Next time, delegates said, let's have someone who 'walks their talk'.

Audiences place greater faith in what they *see* than in what you *say*. So you must always walk your talk. As speakers and trainers, we have no right to instruct an audience to do something that we don't do ourselves. This rule is especially true for managers. It's no good giving a lecture on productivity when your staff knows that a walk into your office will often find you playing games on your computer.

Walk the talk, and 'be' the message. You cannot inspire unless your words have integrity. Effective speakers do not have double standards.

## Use pictures and stories to make your numbers meaningful   39

'For the next twenty quarters, our R25-million-per-annum fund will be divided among 14 accounts, to produce 23% of total growth. We expect a 5% drop in revenue for the next thirteen months, while passive sales of 28% will double at a rate of 10 units per year for the next three seasons, implemented by a ratio of 34% in-house staff, and 66% outsourced labour. I'll be happy to take questions . . .'

Did that mean anything to you? No? Then why do we subject our audiences to similar mind-numbing statistics?

Remember that your objective as a speaker is not to impart information, but to help your audience *understand*. That is a fundamental truth in all communication. It's not about what we say. It's about what they *get*. And from this point of view, it's completely useless for you to have all the numbers at your fingertips if they are meaningless to your audience.

We are communicators, not fact wielders. There is a difference, and wise is the speaker who takes it to heart. Numbers are, by their very nature, abstract representations of actual things. They are *specific* representations, but are nonetheless difficult for the human mind to comprehend in any meaningful way.

Fortunately, there are alternative forms of representation – *pictures* and *comparisons*.

*Pictures* are simple visual depictions of numbers; mental images that people can see and therefore more easily understand. For example, instead of saying, 'R800 million' you might say, 'R800 million, enough money to feed the entire population of Soweto for four months' or 'Enough money to fill a public swimming pool with stacked notes'. Suddenly people have something 'visual' that helps them to comprehend how much money they are dealing with.

In early discussions about the Gautrain rail system, a figure of R13 billion was bandied about. The media soon turned that abstract number into a 'visual' by claiming that it was sufficient to buy a row of S-Class Mercedes-Benzes that would stretch around the globe.

*Comparisons* are like pictures, but they are a little more creative, in that they draw similarities to something else. For example, instead of saying that 200 000 people is 'a lot', you might say, 'The size of the entire South African National Defence Force'.

The next time you are forced to include numbers or statistics in a presentation, try to help your audience to understand exactly what they *mean*. You may relate numbers to something ordinary and familiar, such as the amount of money required for a monthly telephone bill, or for a family of four to eat out, or the amount of petrol they might use for their cars each month. The goal is to associate your amount with something that the audience can relate to quickly while you are on the way to your next sentence. Making it visual makes for swift processing.

# Listen to your audience  40

I was a mere 12 years old when I learnt the importance of 'listening' to your audience. Why? Because I was the victim of a speaker who didn't. And I wasn't alone. I was surrounded by over 800 of my fellow primary school children, packed into a tiny school hall, on one of the hottest Johannesburg mornings in living memory (granted, our memories only stretched back 12 years, and the first three were a little hazy).

It was an end-of-year assembly and a high-level education official had been invited to give us an inspirational talk. He began by telling us that the alphabet held all the keys to success in life, starting with the letter *A*. After ten minutes on the subject of *Attitude*, he proceeded to *B* for *Bravery*. Twenty minutes later he reached *C* for *Caring* . . . And we thought that was more than enough.

But no! To our horror, he kept us in the hall for nearly two hours – a group of hot and wriggly 12-year-olds – until he reached the letter *I*. By this stage even the teachers were rolling their eyes and sighing.

Did he ever speed up? Or listen to what his audience was telling him? Not a chance. He had reached *M* before the headmaster walked onto the stage and stopped him, saying that we had run out of time. We had actually run out of time an hour and a half beforehand and had been humouring him ever since.

What surprised me was how utterly oblivious the speaker was to the groans and sighs each time he proceeded to a new point. It was as if he was stuck on autopilot. I remember feeling simultaneously embarrassed that we were all groaning so audibly at him and annoyed that he wasn't taking the hint. The experience remains seared in my memory. Not surprisingly, our guest was never invited back.

Listen to your audience. Read their faces. Feel the vibe they are putting out. They will speak volumes to you through their expressions, their fidgeting, their smiles, and their laughter or the lack of it.

It's absolutely critical that you consider the feelings of your listeners. Have they been sitting for over an hour? Do they need a bathroom break? Is it too hot in the room? Are they frowning at you, as if to say, 'I really don't understand'? If so, read the signs and react accordingly. Speak to them. Ask them questions. Adjust and adapt.

## 41 Be spontaneous

*Wait a second! What do you mean by 'speaking spontaneously'? Isn't this entire book about how to deliver 'prepared' speeches? Where does this idea come from?*

Well, by this stage I hope I've impressed upon you the notion that a great speech looks and feels like a natural conversation – lively, warm and not at all 'speechy'.

Now let's take the idea one step further – to a fairly advanced speaking technique which we will revisit later in the section on 'Super-effective speaking'(see page 117).

The more spontaneous your presentation, the more interest you will create among the audience – the more *life* you will inject into your talk. Spontaneity is magical, and audiences love it.

I recall watching an episode of Oprah, in which a number of participants had been put through a weight-loss programme. Oprah had the statistics about how each person's blood pressure had improved, but the participants hadn't been given them. Instead she kept the information to herself, then 'broke' it to them live in order to get a natural and 'spontaneous' reaction. The thrill-seeking studio audience lapped it up.

Groucho Marx once remarked cynically, 'If you can fake sincerity, you can fake anything.' Funnily enough that also applies to public speaking. If you can come across as spontaneous, real and natural, you will raise energy levels around the room, and have people listening more readily.

I am not for a moment suggesting you do not prepare a speech. Quite the contrary. I'm suggesting rather that you be *so* well prepared that you make your speech *look* spontaneous; that you consciously *build* 'spontaneity' into your talk.

Now that sounds great in theory. But what *do* you actually do to make a speech appear natural and spontaneous?

First, you must be very familiar with your material. Know your points, and know your stories. Practice telling them over and over again, out loud, in private. Then adopt the following techniques:

1. *Psychological spontaneity*

   This is the tricky part. You have heard your speech a thousand times. You know it word for word. The ideas are no longer new to you – like overchewed steak, they have lost their vitality. But to the audience, they are brand new. Your body language should therefore convey the excitement of developing a new idea while you speak.

   You need to literally *live* each word as you speak it. Concentrate on the *meaning* of what you are saying, *feel* the words, *savour* the ideas, one by one, as you deliver each new line. Do it as if you were hearing the words and processing them psychologically for the first time. Don't rush on to the next thought. Pause. Savour. Enjoy.

2. *Spontaneity through body language*

   In the 2004 World Championships, I intentionally built 'spontaneity' into my speech through pure body language. The topic was 'Heroes', and I was making the point that real heroes don't have to be Hollywood hulks, with bulging muscles, cleft chins and itchy trigger fingers. 'Real heroes', I explained, 'are just ordinary people who make a difference to the lives of others.'

   In order to convey spontaneity, I made a physical show of 'thinking' about my next line, just as though I hadn't rehearsed it a thousand times before.

   I said, 'Real heroes are just ordinary people. Anybody! People just like ...' (and here I cast my eyes to the ceiling, as if trying to think up a good example, even though I knew darn well what my example would be!)

'... like my little sister!' (And my eyes lit up, and my voice tone went up a notch with excitement, as if I'd just thought of a great illustration. Of course, I had had that example in mind from the start).

You can actually build body language into your speech to make it look as if you are thinking up examples, or 'discovering' your next point, on the fly. The effect is spectacular, and it is so simple to do.

You can use this technique in many different ways. Let's imagine you are delivering a presentation on the topic of a new sales technique. Instead of explaining in a tone of voice that says, 'And the next step is, and the next step is ...', deliver it in a voice that reflects the excitement of exploring an idea for the first time.

Let me give you an example of a speech with 'spontaneity' deliberately included at key points. The example comes from a contest-winning speech at a Toastmasters' event.

First, a 'dry' version of the script, which does not include spontaneity points. It contains a minimal amount of staging, but nothing 'spontaneous'. Thereafter, I will reproduce the speech with the spontaneity points included in brackets:

**Example one (no spontaneity points):**
Title: *Look at me!*
(Begin by walking onto the stage, wrapping a glass in a serviette. Stand on the glass and break it.)
*Why on earth do human beings ever marry? Why do we even get together? Is it for the joy of 50 years of the same morning breath?*

*Mr chairman, ladies and gentlemen.*

*In a beautiful little movie called 'Shall We Dance?' Susan Sarandon plays the part of a married woman. In a dimly lit pub, a hardened private eye leans through the haze and asks that very question: 'Why do people ever get together?'*

*This is the answer Susan gave: 'Each of us knows we are only one of billions bustling about on this planet. In throngs and masses, we come and go, hungry to know that we even matter.'*

And so, we need . . . a witness. We need a witness to our lives! We need a witness to the fact that we live and breathe, that we hope and dream. I need to matter. So look at me. If no one's watching, I'm just dancing in the dark.
Look at me!
I've walked the gritty sand streets of sun-soaked Jerusalem, marvelled at medieval castles in France, said my prayers on the stone floors of ancient churches. I've gasped at the grandeur of the Rocky Mountains, ranging from one side of my vision to the other, towering in raw, awesome splendour! Yet each time when I whispered 'Wow!' . . . no one was there to hear it.
Why do we join clubs? Because we need a witness. Why do we make friends, meet strangers? Because we need a witness.
(Stumble over serviette with pieces of glass.) Don't worry. Someone else will pick up the pieces . . . !
But isn't that the problem? Someone else . . . will pick up the pieces.
A friend of mine named Philip once stumbled on the road of life, and no one was watching – no one picked up the pieces. As he grew, his mom bragged about her parental policy of purposeful noninterference, 'I don't have to watch him. My Philip will grow up free, creative, uninhibited.'
He grew up without a witness.
Philip is bright. At 14, he was welcomed into Mensa as a budding genius. I'd like to introduce him to you. But you'd have to walk the streets of Hillbrow to find him. And you'd have to look in the gutters, where he sleeps. And from beneath a pile of yesterday's sodden newspapers, his genius might not reveal itself to you, unless you're selling heroin . . .
Philip grew up without a witness.
I'd like to tell you that a warm hand to hold is more memorable than old castles, and makes a more lasting impression than mountains or cities. THAT'S why human beings get together!
Whose witness are you? Be a witness to someone! So that they will never have to say, 'Won't someone, anyone, please . . . look at me?'

**Example two: the same speech, with spontaneity points built in (shown in brackets):**
Title: *Look at me!*
(Wrap glass in serviette. Stand on and break it.)
(Quizzical facial expression, as if perplexed.) *Why on earth do human beings ever marry? Why do we even get together? Is it for the joy of 50 years of the same morning breath?* (Pause for laughter.)
*Mr chairman, ladies and gentlemen.*
*In a beautiful little movie called 'Shall we Dance?' Susan Sarandon plays the part of a married woman. In a dimly lit pub, a hardened private eye leans through the haze and asks that very question:* (take a drag on imaginary cigarette) *'Why do people ever get together?'* (Exhale.)
*This is the answer Susan gave:* (explain as if this is a revelation) *'Each of us knows we are only one of billions bustling about on this planet. In throngs and masses, we come and go, hungry to know that we even matter.'*
*And so, we need . . .* (Subtle gesture toward my eyes, indicating 'looking') *. . . a witness.* (Long profound pause.)
*We need a witness to our lives.* (Get excited!) *We need a witness to the fact that we live and breathe, that we hope and dream, that we dream and cry.* (Very loud:) **I need to matter! so look at me!**
*If no one's watching,* (Pause, make a show of 'thinking' about the next line) *you're just dancing in the dark!* (Shrug, to suggest 'pointlessness'.)
*Look at me!* (Same gesture as before, indicating 'looking'.)
*I travel a lot. When I do, I make sure I have everything – passport, papers, pens . . . Everything except . . . other people. I almost always travel alone.*
(Grow excited – but deliver in an awed whisper) *I've walked the gritty sand streets of sun-soaked Jerusalem. Marvelled at medieval castles in France, said my prayers on the stone floors of ancient churches!* (Excited, and loud.) *I've gasped at the grandeur of the Rocky Mountains, towering in raw, awesome splendour!* (Stop and think, as if realising something very disappointing.) *Yet each time when I*

whispered 'Wow!' . . . no one was there to hear it. (Body language shows dejection.)
    Why do we join clubs? Because we need a witness!
    Why do we make friends, (Wave hands in the air, as if thinking of more examples) meet strangers? Because we need a witness!
    ('Accidentally' trip over serviette with pieces of glass. Embarrassed look.) Don't worry. Someone else will pick up the pieces . . . !
    (Serious tone, as if realising something.) But isn't that the problem? (Questioning facial expression.) Someone else . . . will pick up the pieces!
    A friend of mine named Philip stumbled on the road of life, and no one was watching. No one picked up the pieces. As he grew up, his mom bragged about her policy of purposeful noninterference, 'I don't have to watch him. My Philip will grow up free, creative, uninhibited.'
    (Change in tone) He grew up without a witness.
    (Deliver next line as if it just occurred to me) Philip is bright! At 14, he was welcomed into Mensa as a genius. I'd like to introduce him to you. (Pause – let the audience wonder whether I am really about to introduce him. Is he here?) But you'd have to walk the streets of Hillbrow to find him. And you'd have to look in the gutters, where he sleeps. And from beneath a pile of yesterday's sodden newspapers, his genius might not reveal itself to you, unless you're selling heroin.
    Philip grew up without a witness.
    (Change in tone – warm and empathetic) I'd like to tell you, a warm hand to hold is more memorable than old castles, and makes a more lasting impression than mountains or holy cities. THAT'S why human beings get together!
    Whose witness are you? (Really ask the audience that line. Scan eyes from one side of the room to the other. Take your time.) Be a witness to someone. So they will never have to say, 'Won't someone, anyone, please . . .' ('Witness' gesture, implying the words 'look at me!' Allow the audience to fill these words in mentally. Don't say them. End in silence.)

Do you see how many opportunities there were for looking 'spontaneous'? And each was planned and scripted – intended from the very beginning. Yet this 'planned spontaneity' gives the speech a freshness and vibrancy that is absent from any presentation that looks and sounds 'rehearsed'.

So always look for 'spontaneity points'. Express them by means of body language, facial expressions and voice. Do this, and your presentations will look 'real'.

# 42 Use rhythm and contrast

I've already discussed using rhythm and contrast in your *voice*. I'd now like to encourage you to build rhythm and contrast into every other element of your presentation, including your script, body language, facial expressions and energy levels.

When preparing for a speech contest, I try to infuse as much contrast as possible into my script. I look for opportunities to move from humour to emotion, from a whisper to a shout, and from calm, subdued body language to expansive movements and gestures. And then back to calmness again.

I'd like to encourage you to do the same. The effect is captivating because your speech never subsides into the ordinary. It is always flowing, changing – like a dance or a piece of music.

The simple rule is this: the more contrasts you have, the more dynamic your presentation will be. The fewer contrasts there are, the 'flatter' and less interesting your speech will be.

We will examine this concept in a more detail under the section 'Super-effective speaking' on page 117.

# 43 Deliver a toast with panache

Toasts are easy to deliver. Unfortunately, they are equally easy to ruin.

Here's what normally happens when a toast is proposed. The speaker will say a number of nice things about the person or occasion being celebrated. Then he or she will realise they haven't brought their glass of wine or water up to the front of the room with them, and will walk back to their table to retrieve it.

Then they will say something like, 'To the bride and groom on the day of their wedding!' and hold their glasses aloft.

At this point, the audience will realise they were supposed to have something in their own glasses for a toast. Half of them will be pouring drinks, and the other half will follow stumblingly, scraping chairs as they rise to their feet. The result is a botched toast.

Then the next speaker will get up and do the same thing.

There is nothing like a mishandled toast to detract from the dignity of an occasion. And yet it is so simple to get right.

The solution is to guide your audience through the toast as if they were sheep. Truly. Control the entire process, step by step, from beginning to end.

Before you begin any toast, ask everyone to fill their glasses. Don't speak while they are doing so – you don't want to compete with the sounds of clinking glasses. Just stand and wait until the noise dies down.

Then, and only then, should you launch into your tribute. Keep it short, and salient. Once you're done, ask everyone to stand. Just that. That's all you have to do – ask them to stand. And while they are busy rising, stop speaking and wait. Don't speak over the scraping of chairs.

Once everyone has risen, lead them into the toast. But make it obvious exactly which words you would like them to repeat. You achieve this by putting those words at the end of your sentence, and by pausing just before them, like this: 'Please join me in drinking a toast (pause). To the bride and groom!'

And to your satisfaction, those present will simultaneously chant, 'To the bride and groom!'

It's that easy. Lead your audience from beginning to end, and be crystal clear with your instructions.

## 44 Maintain control over Q&A

All the way through your presentation you were hoping the audience would ask questions. But they never did. As you spoke, you wondered why they just sat there, immobile.

Consider this: Did you give them permission to interrupt you? Did you tell them they were allowed to ask questions?

Conversely, you might have wanted to answer questions at the end of your talk. But this incredibly rude group kept interrupting you. Then ask yourself: Did you instruct them otherwise?

The way to resolve these difficulties is by controlling Q&A yourself. Decide if you would like audience participation and if so, welcome and encourage it right from the start. You might say something like, 'Let's have an interactive discussion. Please feel free to put your hand up and address me at any stage. I'll be glad to answer your questions as we go along.'

Or if you'd prefer to control the session more strictly and allow time for questions only at the end, you might say, 'Please keep your questions until the end. I might answer them as I go along, but if I don't, I'll gladly go back to them later.'

Q&A is a slippery dynamic, because you can't determine in advance what audience members will say or do. It's often safer not to take questions at all.

Yet many audiences will want and appreciate the opportunity to ask questions. The point to remember is that *you* must decided exactly when and how the questions should be asked. Stay in control throughout.

## 45 Repeat question from the audience

Imagine that you are sitting at the back of a packed auditorium. There are five thousand people present, hanging on the presenter's every word. It has been a superb presentation up to this point, and is now in the question and answer session.

The speaker selects a hand waving from the front row. She walks over to the raised hand, and you can hear her voice over the sound system saying, 'Yes, what is your question?'

But, of course, being at the back of the hall, you cannot hear the question itself. The presenter launches into the answer. But the answer makes no sense to you, because you didn't hear the question.

You forgive the presenter the first time, because she has spoken so well, but then it happens again and you start to grow frustrated. Your mind starts to wander. You turn and start speaking to the person next to you.

Five hundred other audience members sitting toward the back have the same experience. And they start talking among themselves too.

Suddenly the presenter has a problem. She has lost the back half of the auditorium. And she doesn't know why. Up to this point, the audience appeared to be enjoying every moment of her talk.

What she should have done was repeat the question posed to her, for the sake of the rest of the audience. Let's imagine taking a question from a person in the front row, who asks you, 'How old were you when you started collecting East European stamps?'

You should simply say, 'Thank you. The question is, "How old was I when I started collecting East European stamps?"

'Well, I had just passed my third birthday, when an uncle returned from his holiday in Bulgaria . . .' etc., etc.

This simple technique enhances the audience's pleasure in listening to you, and proves that you are a good 'host', not simply a 'performer'.

## Slot in Q&A at the three-quarter mark 46

Very often, Q&A is a speaker's worst fear. This is particularly true for those in careers such as politics, where questions are almost guaranteed to be heated and hostile.

The problem with a poorly handled Q&A session is that it can undermine a perfectly good presentation. Imagine a politician who has given an upbeat account of his party's performance, only to be torn apart by the media and audience members during question time. He closes on a note of evasion and self-justification.

One effective solution to this problem is not to end with Q&A. Slot it in at the three-quarter mark in your speech. This ensures that you don't end up back-pedalling or having to justify yourself. Taking Q&A at the three-quarter mark ensures that you conclude on the note that you choose.

It works like this: Start your presentation. Move into the main body of your speech and deliver all the relevant information, but don't present your strong conclusion. Take questions from the audience, and answer them to the best of your abilities. Answer as many questions as you have time for, and then wrap up the Q&A session.

Thereafter, you are free to bring your speech to a rousing conclusion.

**If you don't know an answer, say so**
When faced with a question to which you don't know the answer, simply admit as much: 'Good question. I'm afraid I don't have that information at hand. Could you give me a contact number or business card afterwards, and let me get back to you? Thank you. Next question please?'

**Ask a heckler for his or her name**
If a hostile member of the audience whose intent is to catch you out asks a particularly spiteful question, don't ever respond with hostility. Ask for the person's name instead: 'What is your name, sir?'

This has the effect of taking the attention off you, and directing it toward the person asking the question. Moreover, the person can no longer remain anonymous. He or she is forced to put their name where their mouth is.

Then thank them for their question, 'Good question, Conrad.'

If they won't give you their name, don't answer their question. Move on to the next person.

### Paraphrase, and get to the heart of the issue

By asking a person's name, you have already bought yourself a couple of seconds to think of a response. If the question is overtly hostile – 'Why, Mr President, do you allow children to starve?' – you do not have to answer the way it was put to you.

The question is phrased in such a way that no matter how you answer, it will make you look bad. It is not an 'honest' question in the sense of asking for information. It is an indirect attack on you.

Your best defence is to respond by first paraphrasing (or rephrasing) the questioner's words and then 'going to the heart' of the issue, rather than answering directly.

In this case, the answer to the question would be: 'Conrad, you appear to be concerned about children (paraphrasing, removing the sting and getting to the heart of the issue). As the President of this country, so am I. Let me address the issue of poverty among children, and tell you what the government is doing about it.'

What you don't want to do is to respond by saying, 'That's not true! I do care about children! I've always said that!' It makes you sound desperate and robs you of authority.

Whenever you are faced with a tricky question, or one that has a sting in the tail, do not answer by using your questioner's own words. I'm not suggesting that you be evasive. But you are not obliged to entertain a slur on your character or an attack on your integrity. Paraphrasing (or rephrasing) a question and going to the heart of an issue is your means of remaining in control in the face of hostility.

# Avoid verbal cues     47

This is another lesson I have learnt from radio, which is equally valid in the field of public speaking.

When you talk to another person, one on one, you tend to provide them with verbal cues to show you are listening, simple little 'mms' and 'uh-huhs'. This is a healthy practice one-on-one, and it encourages your interlocutor to carry on talking.

But I was taken to task for doing it on the radio, 'Because,' my trainer told me, 'the listening public knows you are there, and don't need to be reminded of it. They would like to listen to the answer your guest is giving. Try not to get in the way by saying 'Uh-huh' all the time. It's annoying to the listener.'

The same holds true for an audience listening to you speak to someone in the front row, or answer a question. The negative effect of your 'uh-huhs' is enhanced by the microphone.

What the audience will hear in effect is:
'Mumble, mumble, mumble.'
**'UH-HUH!'**
'Mumble, mumble, mumble.'
**'OKAY!'**
'Mumble, mumble.'
**'RIGHT, YEAH! UH-HUH!'**
'Mumble . . .'
It's awfully distracting (and just a little comical).

To avoid this happening, allow your interlocutor to complete what he or she is saying, without any verbal cues from you whatsoever. You can nod your head to punctuate things or show that you are listening (as I do in the radio studio to encourage my guests), but don't make any audible sound.

Then, once your questioner has finished speaking, repeat the question for the benefit of the rest of the audience, and answer it. But keep the questioning free of any interjection from your side.

If you have the option of offering the questioner the microphone, so much the better.

# 48 End on a 'professional' note

A good ending has three elements: a strong call to action; a decisive close; and the manner in which you leave the stage.

Let's take a look at each, starting with the call to action.

What exactly is a 'call to action'? In sales lingo, it means 'asking for a decision to buy.' One of the most common mistakes in selling is not asking for the sale – hyping up your product, lining up your customer and then leaving, without ever actually saying, 'Would you like to buy?'

Remember that every speech has a basic purpose. When you finish speaking, your audience should:
- feel entertained,
- be persuaded to your way of thinking,
- be convinced of your idea,
- be instructed to carry out your directives,
- be keen to buy your product and know how to do so,
- be educated about your topic, or
- be cautioned against someone or something.

Every speech has a different purpose, but a purpose there must be. Your call to action will simply be a channelling of this purpose into a clear instruction. Earlier, on page 31, I discussed writing the purpose of your speech on the back of a business card. Take another look at your purpose and make it the basis of your call to action. Then turn it into a directive, or 'instruction', for your audience.

For example, if your speech's purpose was to get the sales department's buy-in to a new product and instruct them to start selling it, your call-to-action at the end of the speech may simply be, 'I hope you are as excited about this new product as I am. Take ownership of it. Start talking to people about it. Contact your clients, and get them excited about it. From tomorrow, I would like you to start calling people. Let's each make at least three phone calls first thing tomorrow morning, and set the ball rolling!'

> **Quick tip!**
> Be specific in your call to action. Rather than expressing a vague 'let's go do it', spell out the precise action you would like them to take, e.g. make three phone-calls first thing in the morning. That is much better than simply, 'Go sell it!' The clearer and the more specific your call to action is, the better your results will be.

Now that you have told your audience clearly what you want from them, it's time to wrap up your speech. Untrained speakers have a tendency to become overly formal at this point, not quite knowing how to end off. For example, there is the never-ending ending, usually accompanied by unnecessary remarks such as 'And in conclusion', 'And finally', 'And as I draw to a close,' etc.

To state that you are 'busy concluding' is completely unnecessary. Simply conclude. Stating the fact is like reading out your cues in a theatrical production.

Worse still is the speaker who repeats the phrase 'in conclusion' five or six times. By the third time he says it, you will hear audible groans from the audience. They've heard that one before.

Don't give a hint to what is coming. If you are concluding, simply conclude. You should know what your final, climactic point is, and once you've made it, the moment is over. You've done your job. Leave it at that and do not soften your conclusion with any additions – such as a vote of thanks. End strongly.

Some of the more effective conclusions you might use are:
1. Questions – for example: 'So I ask you, do you have the courage to knock on that door? Will you take up the challenge? When will you begin?'
2. Provocative statements – for example: 'It will happen in our generation. You will see it happen with your own eyes!'
3. Quotes – for example: 'As Churchill said, 'We shall never surrender!'
4. Audience participation – a quite clever technique for an ending, but one which requires a systematic setup during the course of your speech. Continually repeat a simple mantra, perhaps a few catchy words like 'Today will be our day!' Keep repeating these words – at intervals – throughout the speech. Then, you might conclude with, 'When will our day arrive?' – and allow the audience to repeat your mantra back to you. Then sit down.

5. A hanging line – you can achieve a similar effect without inviting audience feedback. In his world-championship winning speech, 'A Key to Fulfilment', Craig Valentine spoke about the value of silence in our daily lives. He ended his presentation by saying, 'I would like to leave you with something that is more powerful than anything I could ever say as a speaker. Ladies and gentleman, I would like to leave you with this . . .' and he stopped speaking and allowed ten seconds of silence, before bowing to the chairman and walking off the stage. Powerful!

Toastmasters International teaches that you shouldn't end with the words 'thank you'. The audience should be thanking you for your presentation, not the other way around. One way, to end, they suggest, is simply to hand control back to the MC, with a quick phrase like 'Mr Chairman'.

I usually conclude my own talk on 'Initiative' with the phrase 'As you choose to use your initiative, and to escape the hamster wheel today, I pray that God will richly bless you!' It tells the audience that I'm ending and gives the cue to applaud if they wish, without belabouring them with *in conclusion's*, or *thank you for listening's*.

Now that you know what types of conclusions are available to you, let's consider your *delivery* of these conclusions.

People tend to remember more vividly the very last thing a person says to them. It stands to reason then that your conclusion should be particularly well designed and delivered, as it will be what will ring in the audience's ears once you sit down.

It would be a pity to have come this far in any speech, only to peter out at the end. Yet it happens frequently. We do it either because we are nervous and start to dash as we see the end in sight, or because we have simply run out of enthusiasm for our own topic or forgotten our purpose.

As you approach the conclusion of your speech, start to build up the pitch, pace and tone. This indicates to the audience that you are about to conclude without your having to say, 'In conclusion . . .' It's like building to a final crescendo in music. It gets the audience listening again if they happen to have drifted off.

Your tone of voice should be similar to the one used for your opening – slightly louder, more pronounced, and with an edge of excitement and enthusiasm.

I tend to script the conclusion of my presentations in advance, so that I know what I am heading towards. Even in an hour-long talk, you can script the last thirty seconds or so. That way you can be assured of a strong ending.

So, well done. Your presentation is over. But you're not quite finished yet. As you walk away from the speaking area, be wary of a common trap. Many speakers assume that people only watch them *while they deliver the speech*. The truth is that an audience is evaluating you long before you begin, and doing so after you conclude as well.

People have built-in BS detectors (that's colloquial for 'nonsense-sensing apparatus'). We are always looking for little cues that give away the character and true intentions of others. Nowhere is this more pronounced than in the few minutes during which you are being introduced, and in the few seconds after you sit down. When you're being introduced, you may feel the urge to fidget with your jacket, straighten your tie, rub your hands together nervously or cough. But don't ever forget: People are watching you. As you are being introduced, their internal monitors are picking up on every little movement you make. After you sit down, they are still monitoring you for integrity. For at least thirty seconds after your talk, you are still being watched.

Be aware of this. When you've finished speaking, walk smartly back to your chair, sit down and place your hands neatly in your lap or on the table before you.

Have you ever seen someone blow wind through their cheeks – 'Phew!' – when they've just finished a difficult speech? Or drop their head into their hands and shake it from side to side as if to say, 'That was terrible. I'm so disappointed in myself!'?

Don't do it. Even if the presentation was an absolute

disaster, don't show that you feel that way. Avoid giving visual cues – resting your head in your hands, shaking your head, frowning, or rolling your eyes. Even if you are a little upset, this is not the time to show it.

Movements like that will undermine your message, and make people feel as that the 'real' you doesn't agree with what the 'on-stage' you has just said. Remember, you are always on show, so give a complete performance.

## Stay after your presentation 49

Speaking and then leaving immediately after having done so is like seducing a stranger and running off in the night. It is more than a little one-night-standish if not plain rude. An audience will often feel used if you conclude and then instantly disappear.

There is one exception to this rule: when the MC announces that you regret having to leave for another engagement, and leads the applause as you exit the room. People will happily accept that you are in demand as a speaker – it can even enhance your credibility – and an MC's announcement will sanction your exit.

Ideally, though, you should stay on after you have spoken and socialise. Not only is it a great networking opportunity, but people will like you more for it. You may also receive valuable feedback that will enable you to perform even better next time, which you would have missed had you left.

Sometimes we have to leave immediately after a talk. The agenda may be running behind time, and you have a plane to catch. If you suspect that you may need to make a dash afterwards, tell the MC in advance, and ask him or her to ask the audience to excuse you after your talk.

If you are able to stay, don't disappoint the delegates by being a different person from the one they have listened to. I quite often hear people commenting about guest speakers: 'He was a completely different person after the speech. I found him to be rude and abrupt. Not a nice guy at all! He had no time for me, and didn't practise what he preached!'

Insincerity can be most damaging to your reputation as a public speaker. It's a matter of integrity – and professionalism. Your audience gave of their time to listen to you. They may have paid to listen to you. To repay these courtesies with thoughtlessness or selfishness is simply unacceptable.

> ### Quick tip!
> **How to kick a speaker out of the room gracefully if you're the MC:**
> I once spoke at the annual conference of a large manufacturing company. They were about to launch a new product. which was top secret, and they planned to do it directly after my speech. My presentation ended, and unsuspectingly, I quietly took a seat in the audience.
>
> The Mc asked awkwardly if I would like any help packing up. I said a polite *'no thank you'*. I would gather my laptop and props afterwards, so as not to disturb the audience. Flummoxed, he stopped, not knowing what to do next. Eventually he mumbled something and asked me to come and collect my props.
>
> At this point I cottoned on that I was being asked to leave the room. It didn't particularly bother me, but the audience was cringing, as they watched me pack up in silence and walk politely out of the room. Someone then met me outside and explained that the audience was about to have a confidential discussion, and apologised for the awkward manner in which I was summarily asked to leave.
>
> If you're ever the MC in such a situation, here's what you do: Be honest about what's happening. All you need say is 'Thank you very much, Douglas. Now unfortunately we need to boot you out of the room (ha, ha!). because we're going to be discussing top-secret industry stuff. Thanks very much for being here today, however, we valued your time with us. Now, while Douglas is busy packing up ... blah, blah, blah ...
>
> So simple. Yet the MC fluffed things badly by trying to be tactful instead of being upfront.

Speaking is an honourable craft, with a proud history. It is not a self-aggrandising ego trip. One of the best approaches I've encountered in a professional speaker came from a lady who imagined, as she spoke, that she had a purse full of gold dust which she was sprinkling over her audience. She was giving them something worthwhile, giving them all she had.

That might sound corny, but it conveys the right outlook. She regards the process as one of 'giving' – of having a good relationship rather than one of 'showing off' at the audience's expense.

# Have an encore prepared 50

It's rare, but it can happen that an audience might ask for more – especially after a particularly humorous or entertaining presentation. And if you aren't prepared, you'll be caught by surprise.

My father recalls how he recited a funny poem at his wedding reception. He thanked the bridesmaids and honoured my mother in verse. It was so well received that when he sat down, people called out for an encore. He hadn't anticipated it, and could only smile and demur.

If you are an entertainer, or if you plan to deliver a particularly humorous talk, keep an encore up your sleeve – just in case. It doesn't have to be long. But it should be snappy – a last, enjoyable morsel for your devotees. Don't ever force an encore if it isn't called for. Just have one, as a standby.

# Summary of action items

Now that we've gone through all the things you should do to become a good public speaker, and looked at the many pitfalls along the way, you are probably feeling a little overwhelmed. Seems a lot to remember, doesn't it?

The truth is that eventually it becomes second nature to use these methods and avoid these mistakes. The more often you are called on to speak in public, and the more you volunteer to do so, the more accustomed you will become to using these techniques. With practice, you will use them without even thinking about it.

For ease of reference, here is a summarised list of the 'actions' described in this book. Use it as a quick guide or refresher before you deliver any talk.

1. If you are not the appropriate person to deliver this presentation, allow someone else to do it.
2. Run through your speech well before the time, particularly your opening – the most critical part of your presentation.
3. If possible, send a short teaser to your audience in advance of your presentation. If not, have the MC drum up enthusiasm for your talk.
4. If a tragedy occurs just before you speak, go into 'dignified' mode. If possible, provide regular updates.
5. Try to be present for the talk just before your own. If you can't, ask the MC about the audience's state of mind.

## Summary of action items

6. Bring along your own introduction and give it to the MC.
7. Ask questions about the audience, so you know who you are speaking to.
8. Ask in advance about the presence of a lectern, and a microphone.
9. Don't begin until you have an audience's complete attention. Speak slowly for your opening four or five sentences. Practice speaking aloud in the room beforehand. Take a glass of hot water into the room with you to keep your vocal cords warm.
10. Spend a couple of minutes allowing your audience to get to know you. Use humour to break the ice.
11. Make it clear up front how the audience will benefit from listening to you.
12. Never say 'just a few words'. Write the purpose of your speech on the back of a business card.
13. Make sure all the information you are presenting is absolutely necessary. Remember to be entertaining.
14. Inject life into your voice. Don't rely on cue cards.
15. Do not insult any members of the audience.
16. Let the audience know that it is okay for them to laugh at you.
17. Build climaxes into your speech, in the form of verbal and motion-based tension. Use the *problem/solution* technique to create a sense of tension.
18. Make your sentences active rather than passive. Speak boldly and avoid euphemisms, as well as long and unwieldy sentences.
19. Command the space available to you by dividing up the speaking area. Deliver each point or 'vignette' from a different part of the stage.
20. Pretend that any cameras are not there. Speak to your audience only.
21. Keep your hand-outs simple and distribute them at the end of your speech.
22. Don't use slides unless you absolutely have to. Keep them to no more than ten, and use visuals rather than text.

23. Speak to each audience *where they are at*. Consider *their* needs and interests.
24. Pause to allow your audience to digest each significant point. Ask either direct or rhetorical questions while you speak.
25. Don't provide an excuse for your audience to doze off. Keep asking questions to engage your listeners. Record your voice to find out how you sound.
26. Avoid visually distracting 'tics' by practising in front of a mirror and being conscious of your body language at all times.
27. Be aware of using crutch words, such as 'like', 'actually', 'okay' and 'um'.
28. Rehearse your speech while you are writing it.
29. Appeal to the imagination by telling stories. Even the driest subjects can be livened up by asking the audience 'to just imagine . . .'
30. Turn your points into stories for easy absorption and quick recall. Collect stories in a speech file.
31. Use 'we' instead of 'you', to avoid distancing yourself from your audience, particularly when offering advice or giving directives. Speak as though on the same team.
32. Speak in the singular, as if you are addressing one person. Each audience member should think you are speaking only to him or her.
33. Beware of paralanguage, and unnecessary asides. You are not required to justify everything you say.
34. Don't overdramatise emotional stories. Tell them tenderly and sincerely for the best results.
35. Consciously use pauses, and write them into your script. Pauses allow you to think, breathe and construct your next thought on the fly.
36. Speak without cue cards, if possible. If you must use them, have no more than four or five numbered cards.
37. Avoid reciting lists. Think more in terms of a creative essay. Lists put audiences to sleep.
38. Be sure to 'walk your talk' and don't allow your personality, or your actions, to contradict your message. An audience will believe more of what they see than hear.

## Summary of action items

39. Numbers and statistics are difficult to absorb. Try to use pictures and comparisons instead.
40. Listen to the cues from your audience. Take careful note and react accordingly.
41. Speak 'spontaneously'. You may have delivered the talk a thousand times, but it's still new to *this* audience.
42. Use rhythm and contrast throughout your speech. Make sure your script appeals to the intellect and that your body language, voice, facial expressions and energy levels vary.
43. When delivering a toast, guide your audiences through each stage of the process. Pause just before the precise words you want them to repeat.
44. Control the 'Question and Answers' session strictly. If you would like questions, say so early on. If not, ask the audience to hold questions until the end.
45. Repeat a question from the audience before answering it, so that people who might not have heard it will know what was asked.
46. Never end your talk with Q&A. Slot it in at the three-quarter mark. If you don't know the answer to a question, say so. Ask a heckler for his or her name, in order to remove the security of anonymity.
47. When you are being asked a question don't give verbal feedback (such as 'yeah, uh-huh', etc.) Simply nod your head. If possible, provide the questioner with a microphone.
48. Don't use the phrase 'in conclusion' – and never more than once. End on a high note – using a question, a quotation or a provocative statement. Use a call to action at the end.
49. If possible, try to stay and socialise after a speech. If you have to leave, ask the MC to tell the audience why.
50. Keep a short encore up your sleeve, just in case.

# Being a perpetual student

My basic approach to public speaking is this: You don't *learn* to speak, in the sense of learning being a once-off course within a certain time. Speaking is a continual learning curve, a *process*. You simply grow increasingly masterful. As wise little Yoda, in *Star Wars*, proclaimed in his deliciously broken English, 'Much to learn, you still have!'

After seven years as a Toastmaster, two attempts at winning the World Championship of Public Speaking, and after a number of years of radio broadcasting and professional speaking in front of corporate audiences, I still have more knowledge to gain than I have gathered already. In this respect, I am a product of the Yoda school.

But that does not discourage me. It's actually incredibly exciting. It's great to know there is more over the horizon. I'm still a relative beginner, and so are you.

That is why, if you wish to become a *great* speaker, you should become a perpetual student of public speaking. This means not only practising, it means *observing* as well. And funnily enough, it doesn't mean observing *speeches* only. You should observe all the performing arts – from movies to music to theatre and perhaps even novel-writing or painting. You should continually be asking yourself: 'Why did that work?' or, if it didn't, 'Why did that fall flat?'

Your mission is to be constantly aware of 'effect' – the effect created by an artist's or producer's desire to stir your

## Being a perpetual student

emotions. If you find yourself crying at a scene in a movie, question why you were so moved. If a line from a poem sends a chill down your spine, ask yourself what it was about that line that hit the tender spot.

Try to evoke a similar response in your own speeches. Don't copy the words – that is plagiarism, unless you acknowledge them – but strive to reproduce a similar effect.

The reason is simple: If it moved you, it will move an audience too. There is a well-known saying in writers' circles: 'No tears in the writer, no tears in the reader.' In the speaking world, we might say, 'If the speaker doesn't feel it, neither will the audience.' Find the things that have an effect on you, and learn to redirect them for your audiences' benefit.

On the other hand, when you listen to a speech, a joke or dialogue in a movie that truly falls flat, ask yourself: *What was missing? Was the timing off? Was it too far over the top? Was the delivery unconvincing? Were there too few highs and lows?*

Turn your 'effects' radar on, and you will be a judge of public speaking even as you walk through a shopping centre, chat with friends, go to church or read a book. Study the effects of clothing, body language, voice intonation and facial expression. Watch others' posture – what does it say about them? Do they look confident, masterful, in control? Evaluate pauses. Evaluate energy levels. Evaluate *everything!*

I do this all the time. My eye is constantly observing why things do or do not work from a creative point of view, and I use these observations in my own presentations, hopefully to good effect.

The patterns underlying drama and art are quite transmissible to the world of public speaking. Emotion, choreography, movement and body language are generic, and what works in one sphere often works equally well in another, with a little adaptation.

Let me give you an example. I remember watching the first *Harry Potter* movie. I was most impressed by the ominous effect created by one of the characters, Professor Snape, when he spoke to young Harry and his friends in a low, slow monotone, using unnaturally long pauses. Leaning threateningly over them, he asked, 'What are a couple of young Griffyndores doing outside on a day like this? (Pause). People might think you were (Pause), (Pause), (Pause), (Pause) ... *up* ... to something!

I enjoyed this effect so much that I used it in one of my own speeches, describing a ponderous radio-station manager, who oversaw my first audition: 'When that little light goes on ... you will be *live* on air. (Pause) In front of thousands of people! (Pause), (Pause), (Pause), (Pause) ... with no erase button should you choose to screw up!'

The second aspect to being a perpetual student of the craft is to practise continually. Professional speaker and humour coach, Darren La Croix, offers three hyphenated words as his mantra for anyone wanting to become an excellent speaker: 'Stage-time, stage-time, stage-time!'

There is nothing like going before an audience, regularly, in order to develop a feel for the way people react to you. The more often you do it, the more comfortable you will become.

Many of the lessons I've tried to impart in this book will only truly come to life once you have 'felt' their effect, when you actually *perform* in front of an audience.

## Opportunities for practice

So where can you go to get extra practice? Toastmasters International is an excellent option.

Toastmasters' clubs generally consist of between twenty to thirty people, who meet either in the evenings, or in the case of some corporate clubs, during the lunch hour. Members deliver presentations prescribed in training manuals, which give clear objectives for each speech. The basic manual, with which every Toastmaster begins, covers fundamentals like voice projection, body language, constructing a speech, and so on.

Once you've worked through this manual, you can move on to more advanced guides, which deal with subjects such as Sales Presentations, Humorous Speaking, Technical and Seminar Presentations, etc. You will receive a grading and a certificate for the training you have completed.

Toastmasters' fees are reasonable (about R600 a year at the time of writing), and include membership of a club, attendance at two meetings per month, feedback on your presentations, a regular monthly magazine from the United States, instruction manuals, as well as the opportunity to forge new friendships and to network extensively.

The environment is friendly and accepting. You needn't worry about being nervous – everybody there has joined for the same reason. Toastmasters' clubs are, in essence, where you can go to make your mistakes, *off line*. The international website is at *www.toastmasters.org* and the Southern African website, which will guide you to a club in your area, is at *www.toastmasters-sa.org.za*.

You can also speak at Rotary clubs, at Lions' lunches, schools, or even at work. In fact, your own workplace is probably the best place to start developing your skills and getting practice. Volunteer to speak on the agenda at meetings, and take on speaking roles whenever you can.

Simply put, the more practice you get, the better you will become – and the less nervous you will be each time. As the man said, 'Stage-time, stage-time, stage-time!'

# Troubleshooting

Here are ways to deal with some of the most common problems you will face.

**1. How to recover from an overtly negative introduction**
Aggressive or negative introductions are extremely rare. But they can happen. If they do, you have a number of choices. Your first is simply not to speak. The second is to tell the audience that you have been set up, apologise, and announce that you will not be delivering your presentation. The third is simply to laugh it off and continue. You might use a line like, 'I didn't realise I mattered so much to you', thereby passing off the negative introduction as a silly, emotional outburst. Whichever way, it's best to remain calm, and not to show that you are flustered.

**2. How to retrieve an audience from the 'graveyard zone'**
The session on the agenda directly after lunch is known as the 'graveyard zone', because your audience is usually lethargic and sleepy. The solution is to be as entertaining as possible, to speak with energy, to use humour and to try to involve the audience as far as possible. It is best to keep the session short and snappy. Avoid long lists, droning explanations and dry content.

## Troubleshooting

**3. What to do when your laptop fights back**
Laptops never seem to work when we most need them to. Ask for help from someone with technical knowledge, but don't keep silent while you are being assisted. Carry on speaking. Be prepared, if necessary, to ditch the laptop and speak without it. Your presentation will probably be the better for it.

**4. How to recover when you've forgotten to thank somebody**
It can happen anywhere, but the most obvious occasion is at a wedding. You've been thanking people left, right and centre, when somebody quietly sneaks up to you and whispers in your ear that you haven't thanked Tannie Hestrie. Don't make a show of it. And don't mention that she had been forgotten. Nothing sounds worse than a word of thanks in the form of an apologetic afterthought, 'Oh, and we forgot to thank Tannie Hestrie . . .'

Just say thank you as if you had been planning to do it all along: 'We would also like to say thank you to Tannie Hestrie . . .'

If you feel you need to justify the fact that someone has just walked up and whispered a reminder in your ear, turn it into something else, 'Gentlemen, please feel free to take off your jackets if you are too hot. Folks, the bathrooms are behind you if you should need them. And Tannie Hestrie, we would now like to say a special word of thanks to you . . . !'

**5. What to do when a cellphone rings during your speech**
Develop a quick, humorous line for use any time this happens, for example, 'Please hold my calls' or 'If it's my Mom, just tell her I'm busy speaking.'

If the phone rings a number of times, stop your presentation, smile and say, 'Please may I ask you to keep your phones off? I've switched mine off. Thank you.'

**6. How to recover if your cue cards are out of order**
Before you speak, number each card in the same place, such as the top left corner. Keep your cards extremely simple (little drawings or key words only).

Take a sip of water while trying to order your cards. It looks quite natural and can buy you time. If you are utterly lost, put your cards into your pocket, and pick up on the 'gist' of what you were saying beforehand.

### 7. How to recover if you lose your place

Audiences cringe when we forget our words or go blank. There is a right and wrong way to react. The wrong way is to draw attention to it, by looking nervous, apologising, showing strain on your face, explaining why you have lost your place, or asking if you may start again. Don't do any of these.

If you have forgotten a word, talk around it. The audience doesn't know what was on your script, so the exact wording is not crucial. Just tell them the gist, the way you would explain it over coffee to a friend.

If you've forgotten the point you were making, move on. The audience doesn't know what points you wish to make, so they won't be aware if you leave one out.

If you absolutely must deliver that piece of information, calmly and casually walk over to your notes, even if it means saying something like, 'Just quickly need to double-check a date.' Find your information, and continue. But above all, don't draw attention to the error. Smooth over it casually as if nothing has happened, and the chances are that the audience won't even notice.

### 8. How to recover when you are inappropriately dressed

Try to make sure you know the dress code in advance. When in doubt, dress up rather than down. It's easy enough to discard a tie or a jacket if you discover that the meeting is informal, but it's not as easy to go up a level.

In a worst-case scenario, charm is your best ally. Make a joke out of it by saying something like, 'Have you ever arrived for a presentation and discovered that you were drastically underdressed? I do apologise . . . May I beg your indulgence and continue? Thank you. Incidentally you all look very fine tonight!'

# Super-effective speaking

## – a guide for award-chasing perfectionists

If you are among that tiny group of sadomasochistic exhibitionists (and I suppose I should count myself among them) who like to make speaking more like a one-person theatrical production, this section is for you.

It deals with 'performance speaking', whether for a competition (in my case, I used these techniques to prepare for the World Championship of Public Speaking), or simply for an exceptionally high-impact, *out-of-this-world* presentation.

Bear in mind that you cannot subject an audience to long periods of high-performance speaking. You will exhaust them, not to mention yourself. But in short bursts, performance speaking can be highly effective. This is how to do it.

## Incorporate 'layers' of special effects

Start by writing out a quick draft of your speech. As a rough guide, 850 words will give you around 10 minutes of speaking if you use dramatic pauses and speak at a steady pace.

Once your speech is written out, begin the process of rewriting for effect. Start with one special effect (for example, focus only on the musical effect of the words), and go through the entire script working on and enhancing only that effect. Then concentrate on the next effect (for example, find places where you might be able to include a dramatic pause), and rework pauses into the script.

Continually rework the script, each time focusing on just one particular effect, until you have finally 'layered' your speech with a series of special effects.

Here are some of the effects you can import into your speeches. (I add them at the top of my scripts to remind me to incorporate all of them, to a greater or lesser extent.)

- **Spontaneity** – As explained on page 87, gestures and motions that suggest spontaneity can actually be scripted and acted out. Deliver each line as if you were enthusiastically *thinking of it* for the first time. Scour your speech for opportunities to do this.

- **Alliteration** – Change a sentence like 'His character was disreputable' to something like 'His character and credibility had crumbled'. Don't overdo it, just use alliteration here and there to add musicality. I remember once listening to a great speech that referred repeatedly to 'The Beast of Intolerance, Indifference and Ignorance'. I remember the words to this day.

- **Humorous one-liners** – Humour can literally be 'inserted' into a speech, using one-liners or through the 'bait and switch' technique, in which you lead an audience down a certain road, and then change the expected outcome.
    Public Speaking World Champion Craig Valentine used this technique in an effective way. He was talking about a girlfriend who had cheated on him and betrayed his trust. He told of how he eventually forgave her, years later. Then, in a friendly and enthusiastic tone of voice, he said, 'Now that I've forgiven her, do we hang out together? Do we collaborate on projects? Do we have fun?' (Switching his tone to one of sarcasm, he said): 'Absolutely not!' This 'switch' elicited laughter simply because it was so unexpected.

You can just as easily build similar set-ups into your speeches.

Another humorous technique is exaggeration. Tell a story (once again, a story in which you are the underdog is usually most effective), and overplay your descriptions. For example, instead of: 'Last night, I got into a fight with a big man in a bar. He was much bigger than me. I didn't stand a chance . . .' you might try it this way: 'Last night, I got into a fight with a man who was eight times my size. He was just sitting there, casually drinking a glass of growth hormone, chewing on a barstool and looking for a convenient punchbag. Lucky for me, I had chosen to wear my Chess Club T-shirt. Now, I'm not the biggest man on the planet. In fact, whenever I walk past a sports field, I have to wear a cap, just to avoid being used as the javelin. . .!'

It just takes a little creativity on your part. Even mundane situations can be livened up with humour.

A third effective humorous technique comes from simple observation. Comedians do this a lot; they pick up on the silliest things that affect our daily lives, such as: 'Don't you hate it when you break wind, only to discover that you weren't alone in the room?'

Or: 'Have you ever noticed that telesales people seem to know exactly when you're planning to get in the shower? I think they have spy-cams hidden throughout private residences all around the country.'

- **Voice work** – Scour your script again for opportunities to use your voice. Speaking is a predominantly auditory craft, so it follows that the more conscious work you put into the 'musicality' of your voice, the better the effect will be.

    I enjoy watching movies with Anthony Hopkins, Jeremy Irons or James Earl Jones in them, simply listening to the manner in which they use their voices. You can learn a great deal by listening critically to *your* favourite movie actors.

    So how exactly do you rework a speech for vocal opportunities?

Look for sections that can be shouted, or delivered in a louder voice. Script them in by writing in 'Shouted'. Then look for sections that can be delivered in a dramatic whisper, and script them in as 'Whispers'.

Look for lines that can be delivered in an especially warm, friendly voice, and conversely, lines where a deeper, more 'ominous' tone of voice might be effective, and practise doing both. I can even remember scripting a section of a speech, so that it read: (Deliver with tremulous and tender voice, full of soul and empathy.) You can also add changes in speed: (Deliver this line fast, with energy!), or (Slow down here; go into a 'chatty' voice) . . . Or a 'contemplative' voice. Or an embarrassed voice. Or an angry one . . . The choices are endless. All this is closely tied to the concept of 'energy levels', as discussed on page 39: 'Build climaxes into your speech'.

- **Vignettes** – As set out on page 44, divide your speech into segments, according to the points you make, or the stories you tell.

  Decide on a location on the stage for each vignette, and deliver it from there. Remember that the front, centre stage is the place from where to deliver positive ideas and 'enthusiastic' segments. The back of the stage is ideal for cold, ominous or 'negative' segments. Script in the choreography of each section, and be careful not to deliver two different vignettes 'on top' of one another. Keep them apart, and use your stage to full and dramatic effect.

- **Acting opportunities** – By 'acting' opportunities, I am not suggesting that you turn your speech into a show. You must, after all, appear natural. But the best storytellers become animated when telling their tales, and so should you.

  I once scripted a section in a speech in which I was having a conversation with someone. At one point in this 'conversation' – both parts of which I acted out – this 'person' said something to me that was particularly shocking. So I turned to the audience, and started discussing his behaviour. But as I did so, I walked around to where I had placed the imaginary character on the stage, and looked him up and down suspiciously.

Here is the script of that section. The speech was about integrity, and it was titled 'One Voice'.

*My hero comes from the glass towers and open plains of Dallas, Texas. I'll never forget what it was like watching Jim . . . as one of a crowd. The audience was riveted. We gave him the applause* (Clap your hands) *due to a man of undeniable talent.*

*But . . .* (Change tone of voice) *I'd like you to join me afterwards in a quiet hotel corridor. The applause had died down. With no audience to witness his words, Jim turned to me,* (Act out his part, talking to me) *'Doug . . . If you ever need any help in future, my friend, I'm just a phone call away. But there's one condition . . .'*

(Step back suspiciously. Turn and talk to audience)

*Terms and conditions? Terms and conditions!* (Rise in volume – accusatory tone) *Was he being two-faced? Was my mentor about to let me down?* (Walk around 'him', looking him up and down) *Was he one of those double dealers who say one thing in public, and another in private?*

(Become Jim again, talking to me) *'The condition is this: Ya must help the next person too!'* (long pause – turn, smile) *No one was there to hear it. He meant it. He speaks with one voice only.*

On another occasion, in a speech titled 'Who Are You?', I began by describing a scene in a gym, then linked this 'amusing' story to my serious message. Here are the staging cues that I used:

*My plan was simple: Join a gym, pack on muscle, and become . . .* (Strike 'cheesy' muscle-man pose) *the ultimate babe magnet!*

*And so, Madam Chair,* (Gesture toward Chair) *friends,* (Gesture toward audience) *I started my first day with a warm-up run on the treadmill.* (Walk over to 'treadmill',

indicate where it is with a gesture) *Just then, an old friend spotted me from across the gym.* (Stand holding bar of 'treadmill', turn and indicate 'friend') *He walked over, stood beside the treadmill and said hello. Without thinking, I turned to shake his hand.* (Turn sideways and extend hand. Long pause)
(Break away from the scene – come forward and talk to audience) *Have you ever tried to run sideways on a treadmill? No? I don't recommend it. The results were as dramatic as they were comical.* (Walk back to scene) *My legs whipped out from under me.* (Act part of 'friend') *He stood there, shaking hands with fresh air.* ('Friend' looks down at the ground, where I have fallen)
*Of course, the problem with falling off a treadmill is that you don't just stop where you land. It shoots you out backwards like a cork out of a bottle.* (Gesture – show something 'shooting' backwards off the 'treadmill') *Lying there on the floor, my ankle over my head and my shoulder in line with my toes, I didn't feel like much of a babe magnet.*
(Come forward and talk to audience again) *There's nothing worse than falling on your face when everyone's looking.* (Smile) *But do you know what's more important?* (Drop smile, change to serious voice tone) *What you do . . .* (Pause) *when no one's looking.* (Pause for emphasis)
(Quick pace, loud) *You see, it's not hard to be a hero when the source of your applause is present and poised to praise you.* (Slow pace, quiet voice) *But true character comes in silent moments, in quiet places, for no reward. True character is what we do* (Pause) *when there is no audience. Who are you* (Pause) *when no one's looking?*

Small acting opportunities, in which you can take on the persona of a different character, or 'demonstrate' an idea rather than simply describing it, can bring your speeches to life. Create little scenarios in your speeches, and act them out.

- **Natural speech** – Having added all of these special effects, you must now be careful not to go 'over the top'.

all good acting, your effects should make the entire work harmonious, but should not be conspicuous themselves.

Each time you add an effect, try it out. Speak it out loud, or act it out in the privacy of your study. There is not much point in adding a range of special effects, only to discover later that they don't look or sound right once implemented.

Also, look for redundant words or phrases and shorten and tighten your script, so that each element has a more pronounced effect. The more words, sentences and minutes you take to express each idea, the more 'saturated' it becomes. Keep it short, sharp and snappy.

- **Remove the polish** – Now that you have reworked your presentation a thousand times over, I would like to offer what will seem like contrary advice: You need to remove some of the polish. This is an invaluable concept I learnt from yet another World Champion of Public Speaking, Morgan McArthur.

    He advises that once you've practised, polished and enhanced a speech to the point of distraction, you may find yourself in danger of delivering an 'over-rehearsed' and therefore 'stilted' presentation. You may need to actually take off some of the polish, and rediscover the raw stuff of your original idea.

Now you have some insights into Super-effective Speaking, let's try to draw the various techniques together. The following extract is reproduced exactly the way I wrote it, including all my notes to myself, staging hints, cues, etc., and comes from a speech which won the semi-finals of the 2005 World Championships of Public Speaking, gaining me entrance to the finals.

When you encounter the word 'beat' between brackets, read this as a mini-pause for the sake of dramatic emphasis. You will also notice that I underline certain sections – in order to remind myself that there is either alliteration or some form of 'music' in these particular words and I should pay attention

That was when the nurse passed by. She waved. Walked across to the other side of the ward, (Cross ominously to stage right and backwards) where the mood was not the same. (Change in tone of voice to 'cold and brooding') The old man, (Beat) on the respirator, had no visitors.

In contrast to the raucous joy that permeated our section of the ward, (Point back to stage, front left) the only sound in his corner was the rasping of raw lungs, and the slow, soft and sinister (Draw this in the air with hands) 'Beep . . . beep . . . beep' of his respirator.

As I watched, the nurse placed a sign (Beat) above his head. It showed 3 little letters: D N R. (Pause. Look at audience) Do you know what those letters stand for? (Nod in silent response if anyone answers) Do . . . Not . . . Resuscitate. (Pause) If his heart were to stop, no one would assist him. His next fall would be his last.

(Walk in silence to centre stage. Switch to introspective tone)

We all know what it feels like to be lonely. You know how it feels when you believe no one can help you. (Shouted) But it is the utter, despairing height of human agony to know that no one will help you! My next fall will be my last, and if I fall, I fall alone. **Do . . . not . . . resuscitate.**

I left, (Two beats) but the incident wouldn't leave my mind.

Perhaps that's why, when I drove home through the heat of day, I was feeling irritable. (Walk to front of stage right) And maybe that was why, when the ragged little barefoot boy with the torn, dirty shirt knocked on my window, (Act part of boy, knocking on window) I turned, barked at him, and rolled up the glass. (Act part of myself doing this) Maybe it was the heat, maybe my mood, (Quiet, introspective tone) maybe it was the light playing against the glass, ('Back to business' tone) but as I rolled up that window, his sign, '**H**elp me – **H**omeless and **h**ungry,' shi**mm**ered, (Draw the sign 'shimmering' in the air with my hand gestures) **m**elted and **m**orphed into three little letters: D N R. That was the sign I chose to place above his head. ('Lift up' this imagined sign, and hold it in the air above my head)

(Long pause for dramatic effect)

Madam Chair . . .

# Speaker's checklist

The following checklist is more comprehensive than you will ordinarily need. Use it as a guide, and customise your own list.

1. **Script**
    Talk outline (script)
    Cue cards
2. **Props, equipment and visual aids**
    Physical props
    Slides
    Visual aids
    Laptop (with fully charged battery)
    Wires and connecting devices
    Projector
    Spare batteries
    Recording devices (audio or video), with sufficient tape or memory
3. **Attire**
    Tie
    Cufflinks
    Jacket
    Make-up
    Polished shoes or heels
    Jewellery
    A change of shirt or blouse
4. **Venue**
    Info about type of microphone
    Lectern
    Size and layout of room

# Speaker's Checklist

5. **Travel logistics**
    Map to the venue
    Contact details of the venue
    Contact details of the host
    Sufficient fuel for your car
    Air ticket
    Hotel reservation and contact details
6. **Audience**
    Find out as much as you can
7. **Agenda**
    At what time will I speak?
    What happens directly before me?
    How much time do I have?
    Am I expected to take questions?
8. **Key people**
    Will any dignitaries or well-known personalities be present?
    What is the name of the person introducing me?
    Is the event sponsored or endorsed? By whom?
9. **Introduction**
    Written introduction for the MC
    Written 'conclusion' (optional – usually for marketing purposes)
10. **Hand-outs**
    Take-home information
    Business cards
    Pamphlets for additional talks
    Press release (basic write-up on myself, with contact details) in case of media presence
11. **Products**
    Books
    CDs
    Order forms
    Sign-up forms for courses or seminars
12. **Emergency measures**
    Headache/heartburn tablets
    Emergency phone numbers

127

# Becoming a professional speaker

## 1. What does a professional speaker do?

A professional speaker is someone whose part-time or full-time job is to give talks, usually on a topic on which they are expert, to gatherings of people. These gatherings might be corporate and 'in-house', public seminars or meetings of private individuals or special interest groups, such as conservation societies, charitable organisations and the like.

Professional speakers fall into a number of different categories, including:

**Trainers** – people who conduct educational seminars, which can last from two or three hours to a few weeks, and are designed to increase the skills level of people in the workplace.

**Motivational speakers** and key-note presenters – who give talks, of (usually) one to two hours, containing advice for the audience to take away and implement in their own lives.

**Inspirational speakers** – who aim to educate, but also to entertain or inspire. The presenters are celebrities, or people who have surmounted great odds or survived extraordinary ordeals. They are usually hired because of who they are, or what they have lived through.

**After-dinner speakers** – whose purpose is to entertain rather than to inform. They may be professional humorists, ventriloquists, singers or nowadays even drummers or fire-walkers. Their speeches are all about enjoyment, hype, laughter, audience participation and bonding.

**MCs (Masters of Ceremonies)** – have the task of keeping an event running. They act in very much the same way as a radio presenter; introducing speakers, creating interesting links between items on the agenda, and generally 'hosting' the event. Professional MCs are often radio or television presenters by trade (though this is by no means a prerequisite).

**Specialists** – speakers who talk specifically on a topic they are uniquely qualified to address, such as politics, science, literature, specific areas of industry or the arts. They are generally invited to speak because they have been highly successful or influential, and are invited to answer the question: 'How did you do it?'

**Team builders** – people who direct the course of an entire event, such as an outdoor activity, extreme sports challenge, etc. Although there is a large motivational element to these events, the job is more that of a 'host' or 'guide' than of a professional speaker. Some team builders, however, are highly qualified in psychology and human development.

## 2. How do I become a professional speaker?

One particularly knowledgeable woman, who runs one of South Africa's leading speakers' bureaus, says she receives calls from people wanting to be professional speakers almost daily. Her first question, and rightly so, is simply, 'Have you ever spoken to an audience before?' With this one question, she is able to eliminate 4/5ths of the hopefuls. The answer is usually 'no'.

The idea of wanting to be a professional speaker, if you

have never spoken in front of an audience, strikes me as absurd. It's like proclaiming that you want to be a professional ice-hockey player when you don't know how to skate. How do you know that you will enjoy it?

The business of public speaking, which has its own intricacies and internal dynamics, is certainly not a 'get-rich-quick' profession. It can be very well paid, but requires hard work, a high level of speaking skill and the patience necessary to acquire experience.

Step one to becoming a professional speaker, therefore, is learning to speak. That you are reading books like this is a good sign, but your interest should not be merely academic. You should get out there and speak . . .

Speak for anyone. Speak for everyone. Start practising and see what it's really like. You may discover that you *don't* like it. Or you may discover that it's pure bliss. But you'll never know until you've tried.

The next thing you need is a topic (or number of topics) on which you are available to speak. Regard your topics as 'products', rather than just 'talks.' Why is that important?

The reason is this: A *talk* can be given on absolutely any subject, such as 'Nail-biting for Beginners', or '16 Ways to Decorate your Tricycle'. But a *product* is something that companies will pay money to hear.

If you want to make a profession out of speaking, you'll need to earn money from it. Unless you speak on a topic that companies or social groups are willing to pay a fee to hear, you will not earn an adequate income.

This is not to say, however, that all speakers must offer topics with a distinctly corporate appeal. You can actually offer a wide variety of subjects, and still be in demand as a paid presenter. The key is to provide either training, insights into strategy, specialised knowledge, or something of human interest.

Here are some actual topics (*products*) being used by people who are earning a living as paid presenters:

## Becoming a professional speaker

- Sales (Lots of people speak on sales. There is money to be made here, but it's a highly saturated market. Do you have something new or different to say that might set you apart from the herd?)
- Leadership (Similar story)
- Communication skills
- Body language
- Effective flirting (No kidding! This is quite a popular talk.)
- Entrepreneurship
- Creating a vision for a company
- Creating a vision for your life
- Trends and future planning
- Scorpions and their lifestyles (again – no kidding!)
- Understanding the differences between generations
- Understanding the differences between the genders
- Time management
- How to become more creative
- How to become more productive
- How to use both sides of your brain together
- How to become a professional speaker (There is a HUGE market in the US and UK for this talk, and there are speakers who make a killing out of talking on it full time, exclusively to audiences of 'wannabe' speakers).
- Lessons from Nature
- Lessons from Bushmen
- Scenario planning
- The classic 'I Climbed a Mountain' talk
- The derivative 'I hiked or swam a great distance, got hijacked, survived a war, had both legs chopped off and got eaten by a shark' talk
- The celebrity talk (I play rugby and have a range of expensive clothing named after me – hear my wisdom)

It's well worth noting that in almost all cases (except for inspirational stories), there is something an audience will *gain* from your speech. They will learn, grow or develop in some way that justifies your fee. In fact, I might even argue that in the case of inspirational speakers, audiences receive both inspiration and entertainment. These are tradable commodities.

So having honed your speaking skills, and having developed a product, your next step is to start marketing yourself. This, unfortunately, is the difficult part. You have a number of different options:

**Speak for free**
I recommend this to every speaker who truly wants to launch a career. Speak for free for anyone who will have you around: schools, businesses, social clubs, etc. The objective is twofold: to practise, and to become known. Your speeches are your greatest marketing tool. Many professionals will confirm that their biggest source of revenue is repeat bookings and referrals; the blessed: 'That was great! Can you come and speak to *us* now?' scenario.

**Write a book**
To quote the exact words of the owner of a speaker's bureau, 'When you have written a book, people regard you as one step down from God.' Nothing increases your credibility, or visibility, quite like having a book in print. And it doesn't seem to matter what your book is about, or whether it is selling well or not. People simply take you more seriously once you have published. You are regarded as an authority.

The second advantage of publishing a book is that you can use it to gain publicity. You might send out press releases to television or radio talk shows, and ask to be interviewed. There are many things you can do to enhance your marketing efforts with a book behind your name.

Some speakers' agents urge their clients to consider self-publishing instead of submitting their manuscript to a publisher. Their rationale is that you may make more money by selling your own books after your presentations than by having them on the shelf in bookstores, where your profit per book is less.

The counterargument, of course, is that a publisher can achieve greater reach for you by retailing your books. And there is an element of satisfaction to having your book 'accepted' rather than simply paying for its publication yourself.

When all is said and done, it's your choice, and depends on the topics you write and speak about, as well as your career goals.

## Develop programmes
This is similar to publishing a book, but simply means recording your content by spoken voice onto a CD or DVD.

## Design business cards, brochures and a website
It is very useful to have basic networking tools, such as business cards, brochures and a website. They help to elevate you from 'some guy who says he speaks for a living' to someone having a serious business. There is something about print on glossy paper or having a web address that adds authenticity to the claim, 'I am a professional speaker'.

Some speakers also develop databases of names and e-mail addresses, to which they send out newsletters. If you do choose to use this marketing tool, you can have a 'sign up' option on your website to grow your numbers.

## Write articles
Writing articles for various publications is another excellent way to market yourself. Generally speaking, you should write these articles for free (although sometimes you might be lucky enough to receive payment). In return, you get to have your contact details published at the end. This is the way public relations (PR) works, and it should never be neglected.

The important criterion is *value* – value for the readers of that particular publication. Although you are using an opportunity to have your contact details publicised, this is not the same thing as advertising. You cannot blatantly punt your services. But there is an implied trade-off: you are offering some insights or 'lessons', which are of value to the readership of the publication, in return for the chance to have your name in print.

You can weave a subtle advertising message into any text, but it must be covert rather than obvious.

## Appear on television and radio
The easiest way to get onto TV or radio is to have a book published. But it's certainly not the only way. Professional speakers appear in the media quite frequently. The key, once again, is the value that you can add to a show.

For example, if it is the beginning of a bright new year, why not contact several talk shows and offer to speak on the topic of motivation for their listeners, as they begin their working year?

Or if there has been a news event that in some way relates to your area of expertise, call the various news services (television, newspaper and radio), and offer to provide an expert opinion. Or you could quite simply send your biographical data (of just one to two pages, preferably including a small photograph), to various journalists and news editors, with a simple note stating that you are available if they would ever like to use you.

You can also get coverage for participation in community events. For example, if you've just set a new record, accomplished something interesting, or been part of a community initiative, contact the local newspaper and ask if they would like to write an article about it. Provided the story is of some interest, you stand a very good chance of getting into your local paper, and perhaps even a regional or national paper.

If and when you are successful in appearing in the media, be sure to stay in touch with the particular journalist or editor, and offer to appear again should you be needed. Keep the media updated on new developments, and you might enjoy repeat appearances.

### Join a speakers' bureau
Seek out agencies for speakers on the internet or in the phone book, and try to get onto their books. You will, however, need to have a number of speeches under your belt before an agency will consider representing you.

### Develop celebrity in other areas
If you would like to shortcut the entire process and elicit instant demand, become a celebrity in some other sphere. Radio and television presenters, well-known actors, sports stars, politicians and famous faces have a really easy time landing speaking assignments. It is a strange truth that in this industry as in others, celebrity counts for more than track record. If you are able to exploit this, by all means do so.

## Network with the right people

A well-known South African sales trainer, Paul Naidoo, once told me that he built his entire career by going to events (sometimes without an invitation) and networking with the convenors. He would make a point of finding out who they were, chatting with them, and eventually selling himself to them as a speaker for their next event.

Every social function provides *some* opportunity for networking. Have business cards at the ready, be prepared to actively promote yourself, and perhaps consider investing in a book on how to develop networking skills. There are plenty available, and there is a body of collected knowledge on the topic that is well worth learning about.

## Cold-call and write to the right people

Finally (and least fun of all), you might consider cold calling, and writing letters directly to the people who might book you for an event. This is tedious, time-consuming and might require a thick skin, but if you are truly interested in developing your career, this is certainly an option to consider.

The most effective form of letter, should you choose to write to your prospect, is one addressed by name (anything else is perceived as junk mail), and which speaks about something relevant to the recipient in the first paragraph (perhaps an observation on a newspaper article concerning his company).

Also, make sure that you are writing to the correct person. Consider very carefully what your speech (product) is and does, and target the person who would be most interested in providing precisely that expertise to their staff. Be sure to talk about 'what they can get' from booking you, rather than just 'who you are'.

It means the difference between headlines such as: 'Marvin the Fantastic Speaker!' and 'Let Marvin treble your sales quota'. The latter is benefit-orientated, and will meet with greater success.

Remember also that with this sort of approach, you are playing a numbers game. The more you try, the greater your chances of success. Twenty letters will simply not be enough. You need to send out hundreds.

## 3. Does it pay well?

Yes! ... *if you can get the work.*

An average fee for a well-established speaker in South Africa, at the time of writing, is around R10 000 for an hour of presenting. This is good money by anyone's standards. But, as with all freelance work, you can't count on having assignments each month, and it takes a long time to build a steady speaking career. You will also certainly not be able to begin at this level of payment. There are speakers in this country who are paid over R15 000 and even above R20 000 per assignment. But these people are usually extremely well-known personalities who are in great and constant demand.

As a new speaker, you should grab any opportunity to speak before an audience, even if it is for free. A reasonable fee for a new speaker might be between R2 000 and R5 000.

## 4. Should I work with a speakers' agency or bureau?

I've heard different answers to this question from different speakers. Some have told me that they get absolutely no work whatsoever from agencies. Others have said that *most* of their assignments come through this channel.

What you should understand is how speakers' bureaus actually work. Typically, they represent fifty or more speakers. They have their favourites – i.e. those speakers who are already bringing in the most bookings. Of course if you are already popular, more bureaus will want to represent you.

Perhaps the best strategy, when working with a bureau, is to ensure that you are worth being promoted. Position yourself as a viable source of income for them, a speaker worth booking, and they in turn will put more engagements your way.

Do bear in mind, also, that you should not rely solely on agents when building your career. They will not provide you

Becoming a professional speaker

with sufficient work or income to survive. Until you are well known and in great demand as a speaker, consider a bureau on y as an additional channel for your career, and not as your primary means of marketing.

## 5. Are there books available on how to become a professional speaker?

One classic, well worth your while reading, is *Speak and Grow Rich* by Dottie Walters. There are many more titles available at places such as Exclusive Books, Estoril Books, and online at *Amazon.com*. Unfortunately, most of these books are imported from America.

## 6. Are there organisations or support structures for professional speakers?

In 2005, a group of South African professional speakers came together to create the National Speakers Association of South Africa (affiliated to the international NSA, based in the United States).

This is a truly top-class organisation, based in Johannesburg, and well worth joining. It provides invaluable support and advice for building a professional career, and each month or so hosts an international speaker who gives a talk on an aspect of professional speaking. The opportunity to meet and compare notes with other speakers also makes it well worth the monthly fee.

You will find the NSA website at *www.nsasouthafrica.co.za*. You can also sign up for their newsletter, as well as follow web links to other NSA chapters around the world.

137

## 7. What is the lifestyle like?

Speaking for a living is very travel-intensive. This can be a perk or a hassle, depending on how you look at it, and depending on whether or not you have a family.

As you become better known, you could find yourself travelling all over South Africa. Some of our top speakers are even called on to speak in different parts of the world, to the point where they might make three or four international trips in a month.

This can be a heady lifestyle. But it can become a bit much if you do not look after your health and manage your personal life very carefully.

The reality of speaking, however, is that it is mostly about marketing. The speaking part itself is undeniably great fun (and the attention and applause can be highly addictive) but it's certainly not the main part of the job. Most of your day will be taken up in marketing your services and trying to land speaking assignments.

A wonderful truth, however, is that the more effectively your marketing is done initially, the less you need to do ultimately. There are speakers in this country who do a bare minimum of marketing, and are still regularly booked, simply on the strength of their reputations. Once again, this is the effect and benefit of celebrity.

There are also perks in the form of invitations to meals, gifts, wine, insights into different industries and different spheres of life, and the opportunity to meet interesting and often important people, whom you might not otherwise have met.

## 8. Do I have to be funny?

The idea of using humour scares away many an aspiring professional speaker. However, there is an amusing, and often-used maxim in the NSA worth noting. It goes: 'Question: Do I have to use humour in my presentations?'

Answer: 'Only if you want to get paid!'

This does not mean, however, that you need to be a stand-up comedian, or develop humour to a high level of expertise. It merely means that you will be perceived as more effective if you lighten your presentations with humour here and there. It is well worth your effort to do so. And bear in mind that you can always re-use lines or jokes that prove effective.

## 9. Do I have to have more than one speech?

Surprisingly, the answer is no. Quinton Coetzee, one of South Africa's most booked and longest-running speakers, has exactly one presentation (at time of writing) and has built an extremely successful career around it.

He constantly refines and polishes the talk, partly to improve his product, and partly as an antidote to boredom for himself, but he has literally been using the same successful formula for well over a decade (in his case, a presentation about the Khoisan, and how they work as a 'team' – as a model for corporate companies to follow).

Realistically, though, this approach suits speakers who specialise in a 'niche' area. Most speakers have three or four presentations, on different topics, in order to sustain their speaking careers.

By contrast with the 'niched' speaker, there is the 'generic' speaker, who can talk on any topic. While you may think that there is some value in being able to talk on virtually anything, it actually softens and weakens your marketing message.

I recall reading an advertisement placed by a group of professional speakers in the US, and being highly impressed with the interesting topics they had to offer. Except for one. This man had an ad that said, 'I can speak on any topic for any audience.' The effect was insipid and unconvincing. What would I actually get from one of his talks? What was he good at? I remember feeling completely unimpressed.

Consider very carefully the value of developing your own niche. Make yourself into somebody special, someone worth hearing. Have a value proposition, which explains what audiences get out of your talks.

## 10. Is it worth it?

*Oh yes!*

There is nothing on earth quite like making a living by doing the thing you love. It is an exciting, fascinating lifestyle, which will take you to all manner of interesting places. It is both humbling and elevating.

You might find the ride exhausting, and you might despair while you build your career, but all in all, it's a magical profession and certainly one that will release you from an office or cubicle.

If you have a presentation you truly believe in, if you are passionate about telling your tale before groups of people, if you have a flair for the dramatic, and a bent for communication, then there is no greater lifestyle. Professional speaking can be awesome!

# Final thought

Let's take a second to chat about responsibility – *your* responsibility as a speaker of any kind.

Oratory is a powerful medium, with the ability to move hearts and minds. Riots and revolutions have been caused by great speakers, and a skilled tongue has led many a nation into the horrors of war.

Armed with speaking skills, you become a more *pronounced* version of yourself – whether for good or evil. Hitler was one of the greatest speakers of all time, and a profoundly evil man.

Use the skills of communication and persuasion that you have gathered here, and from the sources you consult as you continue to grow, with wisdom and responsibility. They come down to us with the endorsement of the ancients. Use them to benefit people, not to harm. Use them to affirm, not to break down. Use them to create, not to destroy.

After all, *Life and Death are in the Power of the Tongue* . . .!

Enjoy the ride!

## About the author

Douglas Kruger is a full-time professional speaker, trainer, and radio talk-show host. He has won the Southern African Toastmasters Championships for Public Speaking three times, in 2001, 2004 and in 2005. In 2004, he represented Africa at the Public Speaking World Championships in Reno, Nevada. Douglas managed to place second in the world. This is the highest ranking anyone from Africa has ever achieved in the history of the competition.

He has hosted radio talk shows on SAfm, Talk Radio 702 and 567 Cape Talk.

Douglas writes a bi-weekly column for the *Star Workplace* and *Cape Argus*, and his motivational articles are regularly seen in various magazines. As a professional speaker, he has spoken and trained for companies like ABSA, Old Mutual, Standard Bank, Revlon, Alexander Forbes, and many more.

Douglas holds a BA degree in Communication and Philosophy from Unisa, and a diploma in Public Relations from Damelin.

List of Books in Print By MINDEX PUBLISHING COMPANY LIMITED.
Tel: 08023453848, 08054755695, 08037404398

| No. | TITLE | AUTHOR(S) |
|---|---|---|
| 1. | Greatest Speeches of Historic Black Leaders volume 2: Malcolm X, Desmond Tutu, Nnamdi Azikiwe, Obafemi Awolowo, Odumegwu Ojukwu, Wole Soyinka, Tafawa Balewa, Yakubu Gowon, Ken Saro-Wiwa | Ben Anagwonye |
| 2. | Barack Obama: Biography and Best Speeches | Ben Anagwonye |
| 3. | Greatest Speeches of Historic Black Leaders: Barack Obama, Martin Luther King, Nelson Mandela, Jesse Jackson | Ben Anagwonye |
| 4. | The World's Greatest Speeches | Vijaya Kumar |
| 5. | The Art of Public Speaking | Vijaya Kumar |
| 6. | Public Speaking in an Instant | K. Leland & K. Bailey |
| 7. | 50 ways to Become a Better Speaker | Douglas Kruger |
| 8. | Speak with Power and Confidence | Patrick Collins |
| 9. | Negotiate to Win: Talking your way to what you want | Patrick Collins |
| 10. | Lifestyle for Total Development | Rishi Kumar Jain |
| 11. | Communication Skills: How to Resolve Conflicts | P. Ahuja, G. Ahuja & A Ahuja |
| 12. | Leveraging Your Communication Style: Enhance Relationship, Build Bridges and reduce Conflicts | John Jackson and Lorraine Bosse-Smith |
| 13. | Relationships: The Key to Love, Sex, and Everything Else | Dean Sherman |
| 14. | The Perfect Match | Dr. Kevin Leman |
| 15. | Created to be His Help Meet | Michael & Debi Pearl |
| 16. | The Necessary Nine | D. Seaborn & P. Newhouse |
| 17. | Before the Ring: Questions Worth Asking | William L. Coleman |
| 18. | Getting Marriage Right | David P. Gushee |
| 19. | When Two become One: Enhancing sexual intimacy in marriage | Chris & M. Cluskey |
| 20. | Lifestyle During Pregnancy | Savitri Ramaiah |
| 21. | Pregnancy and Childbirth | Monika Datta |
| 22. | Pregnancy and Birth Companion | Sister Lilian |
| 23. | Just for Moms | Hoekstra & B. Cutaiar |
| 24. | Just for Girls | Hoekstra & B. Cutaiar |
| 25. | Emotional Phases of a Woman's Life | Jean Lush |
| 26. | The way to Love your wife: Creating greater Love and Passion in the Bedroom | C. Penner and Joyce Penner |
| 27. | How to Become A Mental Millionaire | J.Kohe & J. Willamson |
| 28. | How to Develop Self Confidence for Success | P.C. Ganesan |
| 29. | How to develop a Powerful and Positive Personality | Venkata Iyer |
| 30. | You Can | Don Green |
| 31. | 101 Great Answers to the Toughest Interview Questions | Ron Fry |
| 32. | Unleashing the Force of Favor | Duane Vander Klok |
| 33. | Home Court Advantage: Preparing your Children to be winners in life | Dr. Kevin Leman |
| 34. | First Year Baby Care | Paula Kelly, MD |
| 35. | What Kids Needs Most in a MOM | Patricia H. Rushford |
| 36. | Raising Your Kids to Be Sexually Pure | Richard & Renee Durfield |
| 37. | To Train up a Child | Michael & Debi Pearl |
| 38. | The DNA of Parent-teen Relationships: Discover the Key to your Teen's Heart | Gary Smalley & Greg Smalley |
| 39. | Say Goodbye to Stress | Dr. Kevin Leman |
| 40. | Recovering From the Losses in Life | Norman H. Wright |
| 41. | Healing for Damaged Emotions | Charles M. Sell |
| 42. | The Healthy Balance | C. Allen & C. Winters |
| 43. | Birth Order & You: How it affects Ur personality, Career, Relationship | Dr. R. W. Robertson |

List of Books in Print By MINDEX PUBLISHING CO. LTD. Continues
Tel: 08023453848, 08054755695, 08037404398

| No. | TITLE | AUTHOR(S) |
|---|---|---|
| 44. | LIFEKEYS: Discovering who u are, Why u are here & What u do best. | Kise, Stark & Hirsh |
| 45. | The Eight Pillars of Prosperity | James Allen |
| 46. | The Secrets of Success | James Allen |
| 47. | Money Matters | Slaughter & Miller |
| 48. | Question Your Way to Sales Success | Dave Kahle |
| 49. | 50 Powerful Ways to win New Customers | Paul R. Timm Ph.D |
| 50. | 9 Lies that are Holding Your Business Back....and the Truth that will set it FREE | Steve Chandler |
| 51. | Hands Off Manager | Steve Chandler |
| 52. | 6 Habits of Highly Effective Bosses | S. Kohn & V. O'Connel |
| 53. | Time Management in an Instant | K. Leland & K. Bailey |
| 54. | Managing Time: Plan, Delegate, Manage & Control | Y.C. Halan |
| 55. | Secrets of Closing the Sale | Zig Ziglar |
| 56. | More than a Minute | Holly G. Green |
| 57. | The 24 Hour Turn Around: Discovering the Power to Change | Hartness and Eskelin |
| 58. | 101 Ways to make every Second Count: Time Management Techniques for more success with less stress | Robert W. Bly |
| 59. | 10 Secrets of Time Management For Salespeople: Gain the competitive edge and make every second count | Dave Kahle |
| 60. | Get People to do What You Want | G. Hart & M. Karinch |
| 61. | 101 Great Ideas to Boost Your Business | Kirtii C. Desai |
| 62. | Reinventing Yourself | Steve Chandler |
| 63. | Success With People | Cavett Robert |
| 64. | Riches in Niches | Susan Friedmann |
| 65. | Believe and Achieve | W. Clement Stone |
| 66. | In His Steps | Charles M. Sheldon |
| 67 | Power Through Prayer | E. M. Bounds |
| 68. | The Healing Power of Prayer | L. Tolson & G. Koenig |
| 69. | Miracles can be Yours Today | Pat Robertson |
| 70. | Autobiography of Charles G. Finney | Charles G. Finney |
| 71 | Billy Graham: The Great Evangelist | Sam Wellman |
| 72. | Christian Martyrs of the World | Joxe, French & Woodworth |
| 73. | Heroes of History: Abraham Lincoln: A New Birth of Freedom | Janet & Geoff Benge |
| 74. | It's Possible | Derrick Moore |
| 75. | The Indispensable Visionary | Dr. E. S. Etuk |
| 76. | The Man God Uses | Henry & Tom Blackaby |
| 77. | The Way to Happiness | L. Ron Hubbard |
| 78. | Kill Fear Before Fear Kill You | J.P. Vaswani |
| 79. | Math Right from the Start | Greenberg & Bickart |
| 80. | Study Smart Score High | Cedric M. Kenny |
| 81. | Building Your Baby's Brain | D. Dodge & C. Heroman |
| 82. | Reading Right from the Start | T. Bickart & D. Dodge |
| 83. | Small Changes Big Results | Jerry Foster |
| 84. | Get the Junk out of your Trunk | Duane Vander Klok |
| 85. | Exit of an Icon: Michael Jackson | Ben Anagwonye |
| 86. | The 10 Commandments of Marriage | ED Young |

Copies of these books and other book titles are available at the following Mindex Sales Distribution Centres:
**Benin Office:** 85 New Lagos Road, New Benin, Benin City. Tel: 08033786116
**Abuja Office:** 4 Peter Okunromade Str., Garki II Model Market, Garki 2, Abuja. Tel: 08072250747
**Aba Office:** Shop 112B, F-Line, Ariaria Market, Aba, Abia State, Tel: 08025686984
**Lagos Office:** 20 Bale Street, Ajegunle, Lagos. Tel: 08057377240
Also Available in all leading Bookshops Nationwide